At the Frontier:
Young People and Climate Change

 **UNFPA** state of world population 2009

Youth Supplement

Editorial Team

Youth Supplement to the State of the World Population 2009

Martin Caparros (stories and photos), Dr. Laura Laski,
Victor Bernhardtz

Administrative Assistance
Malak Khatib-Maleh

Acknowledgements

Sincere gratitude goes to the numerous UNFPA colleagues in
Country Offices and UNFPA Headquarters, as well as UNFPA
partners for their inputs provided and information shared, with
particular appreciation to Country Offices in The Philippines,
Niger, Morocco and Nigeria, and to the Regional Offices for the
Arab States and the Pacific, for assisting, advising and facilitat-
ing the interviews of young people portrayed in this publication.

Special appreciation goes to Werner Haug, Prateek Awasthi,
Sabrina Juran, Richard Kollodge, Ziad Mikati, Saskia Schellekens
and Dr. Daniel Schensul for their inputs and support, and in
particular to Marjorie, Mariama, Messias, Kilom, Mandisa,
Youness and Fatima for sharing their life stories with us.

CONTENTS

At the Frontier: Young People and Climate Change

PREFACE

This is the fourth edition of the *Youth Supplement to UNFPA's State of the World Population Report.* This Youth Supplement addresses climate change and young people, through the lens of what impact climate change is predicted to have, and what that will mean for young people's lives, livelihoods, health, rights and development. The Youth Supplement explores these issues because the young people of today will be standing in the frontline in the coming decades, meeting the challenges posed by climate change.

As the Youth Supplement shows, young people will be dealing with the threats and opportunities of climate change whether they choose to do so or are forced to do so, and whether they like it or not. Some of the young people featured in the Youth Supplement have started their passage to adulthood with a strong interest in something completely different, but having identified the issue of climate change and realized how it relates to their lives and communities, they shifted their focus.

Young people all over the world are today standing up and calling for proper attention to climate change. They are both angry with scenarios that in some cases seem inevitable and confident that their contributions will make a difference. The young people featured in this report tell stories that give us a glimpse of what impact climate change might have on young people from different backgrounds and cultures, giving a deeper understanding of how the lives of young people will change, as the projected impacts of climate change arrive.

Climate change is not an isolated phenomenon; on the contrary it will affect young people in all aspects of their lives. The impact of climate change will in many cases be strongest in developing countries, and thus climate change poses a threat to development, as it risks hampering access to water, food, sanitation and security, among other things. Indeed, if we don't implement adequate responses to climate change, the long term realization of the Millennium Development Goals are at risk.

As more young people than ever before live in the world, on the eve of events that will affect them during their whole lives, capacitating and involving young people in the response to climate change is crucial. Poverty, discrimination and gender dynamics are all dynamics that will influence how young people carry out this task. Unless young people are equipped with tools such as education and health, including reproductive health, their empowerment, involvement and contributions will not be possible, or at least a lot less successful.

INTRODUCTION

Climate Change:

"Warming of the climate system is unequivo-cal, as is now evident from observations of increases in global average air and ocean temperatures, widespread melting of snow and ice and rising global average sea level" [1]

Our climate is slowly but surely chang-ing. On all continents and in most oceans, there are observations of changes in natural systems. Observations include, but are not limited to, changes in marine and freshwater biological systems, earlier timing of spring events, reduced ice cover and warmer lakes and rivers. These are all phenomena that represent the impact of a changing climate, but are at the same time only early signs of what might be.

Emissions of greenhouse gas is the most significant, human caused, contributor to climate change. Technology and industrial-ization has provided us with revolutionary means to create wealth and improve health, but our way of life, based on unsustainable patterns of production and consumption,

has also lead to an increase in greenhouse gas emissions by 70 percent, between 1970 and 1994, with the most dramatic increase occurring during the last decade of this peri-od. If the global greenhouse gas emissions are not reduced in the 21st century, it is very likely that the effects of climate change will be more severe, compared to what has already been observed and what is anticipat-ed today. In the long term perspective, it is likely that climate change will go beyond the capacity of human and natural mitigation, if emissions are not reduced. [2]

Young People at the Frontier:

In this year's *Youth Supplement to the State of the World Population*, we meet seven young people who have experienced, or live in the midst of, circumstances that are likely to increase in frequency and force, when impacts of climate change arrive broadly. Among these are floods, reduced agricul-ture production and sanitation problems. While some would say that the events that

the young people profiled in this publica-tion have experienced are clearly early signs of climate change, some would say that it is impossible to draw such conclusions. What is fairly certain however, is that the stories in this publication are examples of what life will bring to millions more young people in the future, if we fail to take action in order to adapt to and mitigate climate change, and reduce carbon emissions.

Poverty is inextricably linked to climate change vulnerability, as well as the capacity to adapt to, and mitigate the impact of emergencies and durable changes of living conditions. Poorer people have less access to water, food, livelihoods, infrastructure, health, housing and services. Hence, a disruption or decrease in access to such com-modities, i.e. projected impacts of climate change, will have a proportionally heavier impact on the lives of poorer people. Further, the regions where the impacts of climate change are predicted to be more severe are often inhabited by poorer people.

INTRODUCTION

Climate change vulnerability also has gender and age aspects: Women account for about two-thirds of the poor people in the world, and about seventy percent of the world's farmers, meaning women will face the lion's share of the challenges in many rural areas.[3] Young people between 10 and 24 years constitute over 1.5 billion people in the world, of which 70 percent live in developing countries. Thus, young people, especially young women, are particularly vulnerable to projected climate change impacts.

The young people of today are standing at the frontier of climate change. Today's actions of governments, the private sector and civil society will determine what lies in store for them, and how well equipped they are for what is to come. A great number of today's youth are growing up in parts of the world where the impacts of climate change will hit hardest; there is an urgent need to address their capacities in taking on the challenges that stand before them. In doing this,

the lives and opportunities for young people must be viewed holistically.

Climate change is coinciding with a current global trend of urbanization. As of 2008, more people in the world live in urban areas than rural, with many of these being young people.[4] This is both a challenge and an opportunity, as urban areas emit high levels of greenhouse gas, but provides possibilities for a more climate friendly organization of waste management and transportation, among other things.[5] Young people in cities are characterized by a similar dualism – they are more educated than their parents, but face greater risks of ending up as slum dwellers, compared to adults.[6] Thus, if young people in cities are to be able to exploit the environmental potential of cities, attention must be given to improvement of their livelihoods.

It has been estimated that in the coming decade, 1.2 billion young people will enter the working-age population. At the same time, over 40 percent of the world's

unemployed are young people.[7] Lack of employment risks leading to a life in poverty, thus more likely to be deprived of opportunities to acquire necessary skills and means to prepare them for climate change effects, and adapt to such effects. Young people's capacity to adapt will be increasingly weakened if their health concerns, including reproductive health concerns, are not adequately addressed. The lack of opportunities and capabilities, combined with the exposure to climate change effects, increases the pressure to migrate and leave their places and countries of origin.

If young people have the ability to take decisions on when and how to form a family, and have the tools to protect themselves from HIV and stay healthy, paired with opportunities for housing, livelihoods and access to commodities such as safe water, they stand a chance of being better prepared in meeting the impacts of climate change. Unwanted pregnancies, sexually transmitted infections and HIV would be less of a challenge, and hence less likely to interfere with young people's capacity to adapt to, and mitigate, climate change. Inversely, if we fail to address reproductive health concerns of young people, we risk making the task more difficult.

New technologies, new solutions:

Because of climate change, the young people of today will need to do things differently than previous generations. Indeed, as generations have shifted over the course of human history, progress, development and the shift in life styles that comes with changes, have always come to pass. The difference lies in that effects of climate change will force the young generation of today to lead a different life than their parents and grandparents, with new set of factors in play, some of them potentially making life exceedingly difficult. The development of new technologies and solutions will not only be triggered by a need to increase wealth and welfare. New inventions and methods will be needed for a

variety of human activities, from farming to transportation, if the young people of today want to be able to continue carrying them out at all.

With projected impacts of climate change, many young people will be forced to migrate, but at the same time, migration as an adaptation strategy to changes has occurred all through human history. While some changes, such as migration, are certain to come about, the manner in which we respond to them will determine the outcome.

In a wide range of initiatives during the past decades, people have sought ways of living that emit less greenhouse gases, are less toxic and function more in harmony with the Earth. Progress has been made on virtually all fronts. The next step must be to make successful inventions available to more people, particularly young people, while making sure that young people are included in the implementation of these inventions, so that they can carry the torch forward, today and tomorrow.

Several of the young people we meet in this publication are involved in such activities, providing examples that young people in all parts of the world have strong ambitions to do their part in adapting to climate change, and mitigating its impact. Young people's commitment to the well-being of the world in which they live is a fact. However, such ambitions must be met by opportunities to increase capacities. Young people should not be limited to being beneficiaries of adaptation and mitigation efforts; we have to give them the opportunity to play an active role in the formation and implementation of responses, if the responses are to be sustainable.

Marjorie

FILIPINA SHELL FISHER
IN WARM WATERS

The first thing that struck her was the space: on the island of Zaragoza, everything seemed enormous, so much sky and light, so many trees. Marjorie had spent her first five years in a slum in Cebu City, the capital of Cebu Island, in the southern Philippines. There, she had lived in a dark room where the only window was a television. Her father had been born there, and her mother had arrived a few years before, leaving behind that island, where life seemed too narrow. But the city was no better: he worked whenever he could in a hollow blocks factory and she did whatever jobs came her way – in a furniture store, in a tiny popular eatery – but there was never enough money. The city was too expensive, because they had to pay for everything – water, food, electricity, rent. On the island, on the other hand, they could build a cabin, plant corn, cassava, bananas and, mostly, fish: the sea promised food.

In 1996, they moved. Months later, when her mother asked her if she wanted to go back to the city, Marjorie was frightened by the mere question and said no, there was no way she wanted to go back. She liked her life on the island. She liked running around all day, playing with her cousins; she even liked it when they laughed at her because she couldn't swim like them: they had always played in these crystal clear blue waters. She liked it even more when, at low tide, they waited for her to teach her how to swim and laugh together.

The island of Zaragoza is separated from the coast of Southern Cebu by one kilometre of sea and coral. The island is a 170-hectare piece of stony land with wooden houses, sparse vegetation and amazing bougainvillea. The 300 families who live on the island have managed to domesticate it, planting gardens and raising pigs and chickens. But the Islanders' main occupation has always been fishing: sardine, danggit, tuna, mackerel, squid and so many others that the men would bring in every morning or afternoon, which the women would sell at the market in Badian, the town on the other side of the water.

On the island – where it is uncommon for a woman to have fewer than six or seven children – Marjorie's parents had more kids. Marjorie started elementary school and, like all the children, soon would go out fishing with her father. Her father and her grandfather would toss the net off of what the locals call bancas, narrow canoes with a rocker on each side. Then her father would dive in the water to scare the fish into the net. From the banca, Marjorie would help them pull in the net. For her it was more fun and play than work: fishing was for men.

But things were getting harder. There were more and more fishermen competing for the catch. And the older folks noticed that the water was warmer and, as a result, the seaweed that the fish used to eat was drying out. That meant that fewer fish were able to find food in the waters surrounding the island. Specialists say the rise in the temperature of ocean waters is one of the most striking effects of climate change. But even before they had heard of global warming, the fishermen from Zaragoza knew that something was going on. It was even harder to make ends meet: many families could no longer afford to eat three times a day and some had to ask their children to help out.

One day, when I was 13, my mother asked me if I could start fishing more seriously, as if it were a job.

"I don't like what they call feminine work. I like the way soldiers are trained and I feel that I can do it as well."

How did you feel then?

I was happy, because I had noticed the hard times we were going through, and I knew I could help to catch more fish. The problem was one year later, when my mother told me that things were worse and I had to leave school, so I could work more and save the costs of studying.

Marjorie's school is public, and there are no fees for public schools in the Philippines: when she speaks of the costs of studying, she is referring to notebooks, pencils, and the occasional book that her cousins couldn't

lend her. For two years, Marjorie and her mother went out fishing in one banca every day while her father and younger brother went out in another. To get just as much as before, if not less, it was necessary to work harder.

Who would get more fish, you and your mother or them?

They would, because they went to the deeper parts.

Why didn't you go to the deeper parts?

Because the net would be very heavy there, it's more appropriate for the men.

After a time, Marjorie was able to catch enough alone so that her mother could stay home and take care of the other six children. During the day, she would go out to fish sea shells: in good times, the Islanders only fished them for their own consumption, but lately they had come to represent an important source of income. Marjorie fishes sea shells in the same way her ancestors did for centuries: the only difference is that she wears a tiny pair of goggles when she dives into the coastal waters to look for the animals hiding in the coral or buried in the

sand. She also has a string tied to her waist, whose other end is tied to the bow of her small banca. If she works constantly for five hours, diving in and out of the water time and again, she can, on a good day, earn 50 Philippine pesos, or about one dollar.

Are you ever afraid in the water?

Sometimes I am. When the water is not clear I imagine that there may be a shark or an eel.

Are there sharks here?

Yes.

Do they kill people?

We've heard a lot of stories.

All the time in the water could however not make Marjorie forget about school. Her cousins had already graduated and Marjorie thought that she would never be able to finish, that she had missed her one chance.

I really wanted to go, because once I graduate I will be able to help my parents send my other siblings to school, says Marjorie, shedding a few tears that she tries to hide.

Last year she and her mother had a serious conversation: Marjorie promised that, if her mother let her go back to school, she would not neglect her work; in fact, she would work a little more to pay for school supplies. Her mother agreed, and Marjorie has finished a whole year. Now she is about to begin her second to last year of school.

I'm just so excited at the thought of finishing school. I was supposed to graduate two years ago, and now I'm afraid that I won't be able to make it.

Marjorie works hard. During the season of small fish, she goes out at night in a larger boat; the only one that can carry the large nets needed to catch those fish. There, Marjorie is an employee who gets a share of the money – and who works, of course, at the same pace as the others. But in recent years it's gotten harder to catch these fish: they always used to come in the summer, when it was dry and hot, but now it rains in the summer too and the small fish flee to the open sea: another side effect of climate change, says Isyang, Marjorie's aunt and the captain of the boat. It is not the only one: before, the Islanders used to plant corn in the rainy season; now, since they never know when the

rainy season will be, they plant when it has rained two or three days in a row. But they never know: oftentimes, the rains stop and the plants die. They can no longer get salt from the sea, another of their resources; the salt is ruined if it gets wet during the drying process. Hence, the Islanders' income has been infringed upon from all directions.

So, in search of fish or sea shells, Marjorie often goes out alone in her banca. And every morning, at seven, she sails to the high school in Badian. If she has been fishing all night, all she has time to do is to stop by her house and pick up her stuff. Those days, she gets everything ready in advance, to save time. Other days she comes home earlier, at around one in the morn-

ing, and sleeps for a while. Marjorie tries to be organized to take full advantage of her time, but some things she cannot control: like that day, a few months ago, when her banca was capsized by winds that eventually brought in a typhoon. Marjorie was really scared but somehow managed to swim back to the coast; then she went home to change and rowed her way to school again. Marjorie really wants to graduate.

If I don't, people will assume that I don't know anything and I won't be able to work in the city.

So you want to go the city? Your mother went there and came back.

Well, that's why I need to study. And I want to go because I want to work there. If here on the island there were fish like before, I would stay, because people lived well here. But now, with the climate change, it's impossible to make a living here.

What kind of work do you imagine yourself doing?

I want to be a soldier.

Marjorie says that since she was a child she has liked the independence boys have, and that she wants to be able to make her dream come true.

I don't like what they call feminine work. I like the way soldiers are trained and I feel that I can do it as well.

Soldiers are trained to kill people, and sometimes they do. If you were a soldier and had to kill somebody, what would you do?

Marjorie laughs discretely and shyly. Marjorie is always trying not to bother anyone, not to call any attention to herself:

Well, I'd be happy if I could shoot before the other person did.

You wouldn't feel any regret?

No, I wouldn't, because I know that if I didn't do it, my mates may be killed by that person.

Marjorie says that, for now, she does not want a boyfriend. She can't see herself carrying around so many children like women on the island do. A small man and father of twelve, Rogelio, the president of the Zaragoza Cooperative, says that having so many children is the ancestors' commandment and it must be respected. If not, the ancestors will get angry, he says. Ysiang counters by saying that the ancestors know nothing about how hard life is now: those were ideas for other times, she says. Marjorie listens in from afar, and smiles. She prefers studying, swimming and fishing with the children from the island to going out with her classmates, "who spend all their time texting and dancing, and I'm not like that." Except when it comes to the cube: recently the Rubik's cube has been all the rage in the Philippines, and even the high school in Badian organized a contest. Marjorie liked the challenge, but she did not have 500

pesos – 10 dollars – to buy the cube, so she had to make do with a generic version that she could afford. That cube was so stiff it was hard to rotate; Marjorie tried everything to loosen it up including oil and shampoo but to no avail. So she started getting to school a little earlier to borrow an original cube from a rich girl in her class who had one. Then the day of the contest came.

It was a memorable day for me: I won. No one expected me to win; I didn't expect to win. I won 5 pesos, and I was so happy! I saved the money to buy something I need or want.

That evening Marjorie thought that maybe someday she would be able to finish school, maybe even go on to get a degree afterwards, and live her dream of becoming a soldier, or become a teacher like her mother wants her to, and go to the city. She says that she will miss the island, her family, the sea, the open space. And that if there were just still enough fish around, she would stay. But everyone says that things will not get better – in fact, they will only get worse, she says. And what can a small person like me do, she asks, in the face of something so big?

FISHING AND AQUACULTURE: WORKING IN THE WATER

Climate change is already affecting and altering marine and freshwater food webs over the world. The long term impacts on fishing and aquaculture from climate change are still unpredictable, but we can expect to see changes in productivity within ecosystems. In warmer waters, the effects are likely to mean less fish, in colder waters more fish. The fishing industry itself is a small, but still significant, contributor to climate change; the average ratio of fuel to carbon dioxide (CO_2) emissions for capture fisheries has been estimated at about 3 teragrams of CO_2 per million tonnes of fuel used.[1]

Poorer people are generally less capacitated to adapt to the projected declines in ecosystem productivity. For fishermen and fisherwomen in poorer regions, which are the regions that will see most of the negative changes in productivity, fewer fish will therefore mean more hardship. Based on the expected effects of climate change, fishing will need to be undertaken in more extreme weather, farther from land, and require more human resources. More working hours and more fuel will be needed in order to gather the necessary catch.

In areas where fisheries are a substantial part of the economy, climate change will affect a great number of people. In the Lower Mekong area for example, two thirds of the population, or 60 million people, are in some way working in fisheries, or in sectors related to fisheries. Their work and living by the Mekong will change as the Mekong is expected to change, due to altered patterns of precipitation, snowmelt, and rising sea levels. While it is difficult to give exact estimates of what will happen, a sea level rise of 20 cm would, according to models, lead to dramatic changes in species in the Lower Mekong Delta.[2]

While changes in species might not necessarily lead to a decrease in the amount of catch available, a loss of biological diversity may have health implications for humans. Research suggests that tropical diseases posing a threat to humans are buffered by the diversity of species that exist in tropical countries. A decrease in biological diversity hence means a risk in increased spread of tropical diseases. Many argue that such diseases are responsible for the lion's share of tropical countries' economic challenges.[3] One of these diseases is the hookworm infection, considered a neglected tropical disease, causing childhood and maternal anaemia, which risks leading to disabilities.[4]

As the story of Marjorie shows, young girls in developing countries are often involved in agricultural work and work to support the home, such as gathering fuel and carrying water, instead of staying in school. For families who work in the informal agriculture sector, taking children from school to the farm is often necessary. It is important to note however, that in developing countries, children's contribution to a family's yield are often insignificant in the efforts to lift the family out of poverty, since children lack necessary training and experience. In addition, children are more vulnerable as agriculture workers. The agriculture sector is counted among the top three dangerous sectors in which to work, in terms of the number of work-related deaths, accidents and cases of occupational disease and ill health.[5] In South-East Asia, many poor families rely heavily on small-scale agricultural fishing for their livelihoods, and with effects of climate change starting to show, they identify new threats to their already fragile positions.

As women and young people make up a large share of fisher people, ensuring that small-scale fishing survives, through enhancing the capacities of women and young people to carry out their work, is crucial in the face of climate change. At the same time, initiatives that make it possible for children and young people, particularly adolescent girls, in fisher families to enroll in education, are imperative. Adolescent girls without education or only primary education face higher risks of unwanted and/or unsafe pregnancy, lack of sustainable livelihoods and lack of opportunities for empowerment.[6]

Mariama

NIGERIEN CEREAL BANK MEMBER
EARNING RESPECT AND SECURING FOOD

Mariama has a husband, three children, dozens of relatives, an adobe hut with a straw roof, a few hens, five dresses, some colourful scarves, a mortar, a hoe, a dozen plates and cups, some spoons, four pots, some jerricans, four light bulbs, three bracelets and a very pretty necklace. Mariama knows that she was born in 1983, but she does not know the exact date – and it never occurred to her that she should know it.

Niger is one of the poorest nations in the world, a very large country full of desert; the birth rate of its 15 million inhabitants – 83 percent are farmers – is among the highest on the planet: 7.7 children per woman. Mariama was born in Dokimana, a town with no electricity or running water about 60 kilometres from Niamey, the capital city – where her father worked two or three hectares of land. Mariama was the fifth of seven siblings, so she always had someone to play with around the house or near the river. When she was six, she began helping around the house: she would help her mother cook,

clean, bring water in from the well and firewood down from the bush. She also helped her mother with her crops: women often grow gombo, a common local condiment, on their own.

Her parents never sent her to school. Her brothers went, but she didn't, and now she regrets it: she believes that, had she gone, she would have had more opportunities, like some of her neighbours who became teachers and earn a salary and don't spend their lives grinding millet. When she was ten though, her mother and grandmother started to teach her the Koran: Mariama learned to recognize those letters and, after a time, she was able to remember and reproduce sounds that, together, made sentences in Arabic which she, of course, did not understand. It was like singing a song whose lyrics, she had been told, were the word of God. Later, each night at the town's Koranic school, by the light of oil lanterns, the marabou – the religious wise man – would explain to her what the words she was repeating meant.

What did you most like doing when you were a teenager?

What I most liked doing was filling up my belly, getting dressed up and reading the Koran.

Ten years ago, when Mariama was sixteen, a man from Dalweye, thirty kilometres away, came to Dokimana: his name was Aboubakar. He was twenty-five years old and had some relatives there and, it later became clear, he was looking for a wife. One day, the man walked up to Mariama, looked her straight in the eye, and told her that he loved her. Then he went back to his town to tell his parents that he had found his wife.

Here, we don't spend a lot of time conversing, dating, stuff like that. If a boy wants to marry a girl and the girl agrees, they get married as soon as they can prepare the wedding.

Dalweye is a very poor town, a hundred adobe constructions scattered on dry ground. Mariama was afraid: she was no longer under the control of her father but of her husband, and she was going to spend the rest of her life with a man whom she barely knew in a place that was not her own.

Weren't you happy to get married?

No, well, yes... I knew that I could trust my husband, he was not a stranger to my family. But the man is always stronger than the woman, and you never know what will happen.

"I also see myself differently, because I know that I make a contribution to the household."

Mariama became a wife: she cleaned the house, ground the grain, washed, cooked, and went to the fields to take her husband millet paste for lunch. One year later, she had her first child; the girl was born at home under the care of the town midwife. She had a normal life full of hard work; it might have been calm if there were not the constant threat of hunger.

Mariama's family – and most Nigerien farmers – eat, if they can, three times a day: at dawn, a ball made out of millet that has been ground for hours in a wooden mortar, mixed with a little milk or water; at midday, the same millet dish or a soup that consists of hot water with millet flour. Dinner, when night falls, is the most elaborate meal: it consists of millet or corn paste with a sauce made from baobab leaves, gombo or whatever there is. Two or three times a month they also eat fish, or some chicken. And on holidays or special occasions, Mariama makes white rice with a sauce made from sorrel, squash, tomato and peanut paste.

But sometimes we don't have much food, and we can only eat twice, or even once, a day. Or we don't have anything at all.

The most difficult time of year is the period they call "la soudure". In June, when the rains start, the peasants plant millet and corn to be harvested in October; those months when the earlier harvest is running out and the next one has not yet begun – especially August and September – are times of hunger. Mariama has always known hardship, but the situation is getting worse every year.

Before, an average field, three or four hectares, could yield up to 300 heaps of millet. Now, if it yields 150 that's a lot. And before each heap yielded seven or eight tias, and now they never yield more than three.

The most common measure in Niger, a tia, is a bowl that contains two and a half kilos of grain. And Mariama says that the grains don't ripen because the lands are used up, the fertilizer is very expensive and there are no carts to bring it in. And there are few trees left because they have been chopped down for firewood and to build houses and utensils – "If you don't have wood, you can't do anything here" – and that, since there are no plants, there is less water. But the worst thing is that now it rains much less than before, she says, less and less. Without naming it – she wouldn't know the name –, Mariama speaks of climate change.

In 1999, when she arrived to Dalweye, Mariama found out that some women there had started a support group. In Mariama's town nothing like that existed and at first, a shy newcomer, she didn't dare ask them to let her in. But she did follow their activities. The first group of women from Dalweye was formed in 1997 following a Care International initiative. It consisted of forty women who got together, talked about their problems and tried to contribute 100 francs – about 20 US cents – every week to build a fund that would offer them loans of 5,000 to 10,000 francs to help start up a small business: selling fritters, couscous, milk. The group helped them to get by, but eventually they learned out about cereal banks, and wanted to form one.

Cereal banks are one of the most efficient ways to fight the threat of hunger following droughts in Niger. There are already 2,000 cereal banks in the country. The mechanism is simple: a group of women who have been active in their villages commits to build a warehouse, and they receive from the World Food Programme – through different NGOs – an initial capital in the form of grain, usually one hundred 100-kilo sacks of millet, corn and rice.

The bank sells and/or lends small amounts of grain to the community at two key times of year: in the month of June, when the first rains say that it is time to plant, and when "la soudure" comes. The women, who are divided into commissions, run the bank, though all the major decisions are made in a general assembly. In order to be sustainable, the bank annually "capitalizes", and buys more grain for the following year. Through the bank, women are able to get grain in their hometowns, instead of

having to walk dozens of kilometres to the nearest market. The bank also regulates prices, since the bank's prices are always below the market. Primarily though, the bank is a resource that reduces the threat of hunger, and earns women a place of respect in their communities and homes.

Now my husband looks at me differently. He knows that without the bank we sometimes would have nothing to eat, and we women are the bank. I also see myself differently, because I know that I make a contribution to the household.

In 2002, the women from Dalweye joined all their resources to build the warehouse. They say proudly that they did it by themselves.

No, we men helped out, says a representative of the village chief.

You did some work, but we women provided the money.

Amidst laughter, the debate at the Dalweye women's assembly carries on. They have gathered this morning at the hirara – "the place of the words" in Djerma – under the mango tree to discuss the figures for the last year. The president shows them the books: they have 821,930 francos in cash and 153 100-kilo sacks of grain. Mariama sits among the women. She joined the group seven years ago, when the warehouse was being built, and now she participates in all of its activities: discussions, debates, training classes, and a literacy course. When "la soudre" comes round, Mariama often buys grain: a few years ago, the women from Dalweye decided not to make any more cereal loans because it often took them too long to get them back and that created problems.

In 2005, electricity came to Dalweye. Before, night in the town was gloomy and silent; now people don't have to go to bed when it gets dark. And the mill works better, and some people even have a fridge to cool water to sell. Mariama only uses electricity to light her house with a few light bulbs: that's the only electrical gadget she has.

That year, Mariama had her first son, and she was very relieved. A boy can help his father in the fields and, when he gets married, he doesn't leave but brings his wife home; the boy's mother can finally rest as her daughter-in-law does the housework. A son is labour and the promise of retirement. And Mariama knew that women who do not produce male offspring can be scorned by their husbands. Indeed, if they can, such husbands may take a second wife, because they never believe it could be their fault that they don't have male children.

Mariama's life varies little from day to day. She gets up with the sun every morning, goes to the well to get water, makes breakfast, sends her children to school, dusts the house, grinds the millet, talks to her relatives, cooks the midday millet, takes it to her husband, tends to her small lot of gombo, washes the clothes, looks after the children, makes dinner and goes to bed. She sometimes sells couscous outside the school.

Is there ever a day when you don't work?

No, why?

Just asking.

No. Only when I am sick. But if not, no, I work every single day.

And would you like not to work one day?

Yes, I would. But I know that is never going to happen. Well, maybe when my children are grown up, but not before.

Mariama thinks that if her children learn how to read and write, even to speak a little French, maybe when they are grown up they will have a trade and, perhaps, even be able to support her.

Have you ever been to Niamey?

Yes, I have been there to see relatives. I like it very much. The food is good, and you can tell that people are well fed. They are attractive and clean, their skin is shiny and their clothing pretty. The poor people in the city are better off than the rich people here.

Would you like to live there?

Yes, of course.

Why not try?

Because we don't have enough money to live there. There you have to have a lot of money, because you have to pay for everything: wood, water, food, everything is for sale.

And if one day a magician came along and told you could be whatever you wanted and do whatever you liked, what would you choose?

What I want is to have enough money to buy some cows and fatten them up, to plant spices and sell them at the market, to have a fridge to cool water and sell it, to really start a business. That's what I would choose to do. To know that I will never go hungry.

DROUGHT AND DESERTIFICATION
FARMING A WARMER EARTH

In the coming century, regions in the world regularly experiencing droughts and heat waves are likely to experience more frequent extreme weather conditions because of climate change. Further, vulnerability to droughts, in both developing and developed countries, is estimated to be higher than previously believed, based on observation of recent events.[1]

As Mariama's story shows us, many women assume farming responsibilities at an early age. But her story also shows us that there are ways to safeguard the availability of seeds and food while empowering women, including young women. This is important, as experts suggest that the management of drylands will only be successful when men and women participate fully and equally in the work.[2]

A dryer land affects both rural and urban populations, with the impact being more difficult to mitigate for poor people and people living in drylands. Agriculture will suffer not only from smaller yields, through weaker soil, lack of water and damage to crops, but also threats such as increased death in livestock and more frequent wild fires. Cities will suffer from lack of access to water and water pollution, bringing sanitation problems as well as shortage in water needed in industry and construction. People living in cities can expect a magnified extent of droughts and heat waves, as cities are hotter than nearby rural areas. The risk of spreading of food- and waterborne diseases increases.[3]

The toll of more frequent and stronger droughts and heat waves will be both human and economic. Although current droughts are not all associated with climate change, analyzing their effects hints as to why mitigation of the effects of droughts is essential. In West Africa, long droughts have forced some nomad populations to settle down, radically transforming centuries-old ways of living and forcing people to learn new methods of farming and caring for their cattle. While there might be no alternatives to such change, initiatives to strengthen the capacities of former nomad populations are crucial, and need to be sensitive to what the change might mean culturally.

More frequent and stronger droughts and heat waves also risk having vast impacts on biodiversity and desertification. Desertification; the degradation of land in arid, semi-arid, and dry sub-humid areas (not the expansion of existing deserts), occurs when a number of factors interplay: One is the removal of forest and plants from land (to be used as fuel or giving way to farming, new construction and urban expansion), as it means there is nothing binding the soil any longer. Another is eroding of topsoil through herding of cattle. A third is overexploitation of soil through farming.[4]

All of these factors relate to poverty and lack in capacity to sustainably farm the land. About 90 percent of the worlds dryland populations live in developing countries. Wind and water erosion enhances the process, leaving the land in a mix of sand and dust. Drought and heat waves amplify the process. Currently, as much as 40 percent of the earth's land is threatened by desertification.[5]

Desertification does not only bring challenges in terms of food shortage, sandstorms or disruption of water flows; it is also a serious challenge in terms of security. Desertification risk triggering crisis in regions characterized by famine, political and civil unrest, migration and war.[6] It also has a gender dimension. Traditionally, agriculture work in drylands is heavily gender-segregated, with women assuming large responsibilities for gathering and preparing food. Thus, women's status and livelihoods are jeopardized when droughts and desertification threatens access to food. Women's socio-economic status is therefore a component that must be included in work aiming at adapting to and mitigating the effects of drought and desertification.[7] Further, it is essential that both men and women are involved in initiatives that potentially change power dynamics, if changes are to be accepted by the community as a whole and persevere. Mariama's experiences stand as an important example.

The term drought may refer to a meteorological drought (precipitation well below average), hydrological drought (low river flows and low water levels in rivers, lakes and groundwater), agricultural drought (low soil moisture), or environmental drought (a combination of the above). The impact of a drought is dependent on human behaviour, such as how land is used, how water resources are exploited and the size of the population living off a specific water source.[8]

Messias

AMAZONIAN COMMUNITY PRESIDENT
PERMACULTURE PIONEER

It all started as a joke: "This kid talks so much he should be president; yeah, he doesn't stop, he's like a fish out of water," the older folks would say. But, one joke at a time, they started to take him seriously. A few months later Messias, at the time age twelve, fifth child of Maria and Raimundo, was elected president of the community of Sant'Antonio, on the island of Urubú, district of Boa Vista do Ramos, state of Amazonas, Brazil.

The Amazon is the largest green reserve on the planet: five and a half million square kilometres – divided between Brazil, Bolivia, Peru, Ecuador, Colombia, Venezuela and Guyana – that house much of the world's biodiversity and reabsorb large amounts of CO_2, reducing the greenhouse effect. The Amazon also has a great influence on the climate of the whole continent. But, in the last forty years, ever faster deforestation to plant soy and raise cattle has devastated more than 500.000 square kilometres of forests.

Messias was born on December 5, 1984 –"or was it 83? Truth is, I can't remember" – in a straw-roofed hut next to the river; his father worked for a local landowner. In a world where most are newly arrived settlers, Messias's parents are Amazon natives, children of Amazon natives, landless Caboclos. Messias grew up watching his siblings go away: there was not enough money and, one by one, the older children had to leave to make a living. They worked as sailors on the river, and they always sent something back home. Messias was like an only child; his illiterate father would take him along when he worked the land, and would always tell him that he must not depend on bosses and merchants: to be free, he had to be able to produce his own food. Some nights they would go into the woods to hunt venison, giant armadillo, paca and tapir – which still abounded – and he would teach Messias everything he knew about plants and animals. Or they would go fishing with bow and arrow – "that's right, like Indians" – with a net, with harpoons. By the time Messias started school, he knew a lot about the river, the jungle and the crops.

Urubú is a secluded and isolated zone to which there is no land access; few boats make it there. There was no electricity and the pace of people's life was – and still is – set by sunlight. Messias was six or seven years old the first time his parents took him to a city, to see a doctor. He was shocked: he had never before seen a paved road, a car, a two-storey house, street lights, those markets full of objects, fruits and vegetables.

At that time Messias also came across that strange creature that his richest neighbours had brought from faraway: a television. Full of wonder, the locals would gather in front of the gadget to watch soccer matches. Each one put in fifty cents to pay for diesel for the generator; the ones who didn't have any money could also watch through the window, but everyone wanted to stick his nose up against the screen.

It was amazing. Before, it was just radio, radio, and more radio. You could listen but you could not see anything.

Soccer was an important part of his life: every Saturday and Sunday, the whole community would gather around the field for a game, a little bit of music, conversation and some beer. Messias was twelve by then, and he spent the whole time talking to people: he told them that they should produce their own food to keep from depending on cities, that they could grow crops closer to their houses so as not to walk so much. In the Amazon, it is common to use a slash-and-burn system that produces a great deal of CO_2 – contributing to global warming and wearing out the soil. Under this system, each parcel can be used for two years and then must lie fallow for six or seven, so the

"...I tell them we have to take care of it. It's not just us, the whole world needs the Amazon."

peasants can't harvest as much as they need. In fact, eighty percent of the food consumed in the "lungs of the Earth" is brought in from elsewhere.

Messias's neighbours listened to him: in the next election, Messias defeated one of his cousins – on the island everyone is more or less related – and was elected president of the community.

The president is the person who organizes the community and its relations with the authorities. He also looks after the common property, makes sure that every member is contributing, organizes the Saint's celebration, ensures cleanliness, keeps track of the teachers' work, mediates between neighbours.

Many preferred to do things right from the get-go rather than withstand the shame of being scolded by a kid like me...

At first, Messias was afraid of not doing a good job or of being ignored; little by little, though, he learned and gained confidence. Times were hard: his father's boss had fired him for no reason after forty years on the job. Raimundo sued, but meanwhile, money was tight: Messias went to work on other ranches, fished for food, and grew desperate.

When he was eighteen, his girlfriend got pregnant and they had their first child, but Messias did not want to move in with her. By that time, his father had received as severance pay the land where they had always lived, and Messias was able to attend the agro-technical school on the island. That's where he met the people from the Instituto de Permacultura do Amazonas, based in

Manaos, who wanted to start up a project in the countryside.

Permaculture – or permanent agriculture – is the science of the obvious: observing nature in order to learn how to produce food without destroying it, says Carlos Miller, who, along with Ali Sharif, founded the Instituto in 1997.

It means coming up with systems of sustainable crops where all the components are interrelated and benefit each other, because everything is connected: permaculture is not about the soil, the trees, the rain, the sun, the animals, but the connections between them. We always say that no element performs just one function: they all have several, and you have to know how to combine them. The idea is to create a new equation for wealth in the Amazon in order to preserve the region: wealth that does not mean destruction,

Before the Instituto, Miller had worked in ecological NGOs that, in order to protect certain areas, emptied them out:

I was not comfortable with that: how was it possible that, in order to save a piece of

land, it was necessary to expel the people who lived on it. When I learned about permaculture, I thought it might be a solution. When man plants, he removes everything he finds and plants in the vacuum he has created. The Amazon forest does just the opposite, because it rests on land that has few nutrients, and needs to live off of itself, of its own decomposition. We copy that system, using natural fertilizers and combining plants that help each other grow without destroying the environment.

Messias was excited: he thought that this could be a solution for his people. Miller told him to keep studying to prove to him that his interest was real. When he graduated, in October of 2004, Messias went on to study at the Instituto de Manaos that – in conjunction with the district of Boa Vista – was putting together the Proyecto Casa Familiar Rural on the island of Urubú. The project was run by Genice, a young indigenous woman. In 2006, Ali and Carlos invited Messias to join in.

Now, the project revolves around a large cabin in the middle of a hectare – just one hectare – full of resources: more than one hundred varieties of productive plants: corn, cassava, sugar cane, rice, onion, banana, coffee, pineapple, avocado, chestnut, passion fruit, guava, açaí palm and many others. There is also a greenhouse to grow more plants; chicken and quail coops for eggs and fertilizer; a system to gather and filter rain water; solar energy panels; a compost-producing toilet. In a pond fish are bred, and there will soon be a pigsty whose detritus will be turned into methane gas. The project has to be self-sustaining and, above all, it has to serve as a model to further community development by showing the neighbours that they can survive without wasting so much energy and time, and so many natural resources.

It's not easy, because of their culture: burning, planting and fishing. When you tell them that they can produce without burning, without destroying nature, some tell you you're crazy or ignorant, says Messias, sitting at the entrance to the hut where he has always lived.

One of the problems, he says, is that the communities in the area are too used to public assistance. A few months ago, for instance, the project built and furnished a chicken coop in a nearby community. Shortly after finishing, the neighbours sold the chickens and asked them to buy them more.

They are very dependent. If no one is pushing them, they spend the whole day gazing up at the sky, passing the time. I try to tell them that they have to do things on their own, for themselves, but it's still me saying it. Anyway, that's our role here: showing them that it's not necessary to burn to raze the woods or to fish with nets. Some of them understand and put it into practice. Fewer people burn the woods, more people fish more carefully. They have banned fishing in certain lakes. People have started planting gardens and fruit trees, and beekeeping. We want this region of the Urubú River to be an example for other communities, so that they can see how our lives improve and how they can apply and spread these practices in their areas.

Messias is still very enthusiastic but he knows that many are opposed to the model: the ranchers, because they want more land for cattle; the merchants, because if the peasants produce their own food, they won't buy it from them. Messias looks to the government for help and tries to explain to his countrymen that if they don't preserve nature they will lose everything. He tells them that preserving nature is their duty as Amazonians, because the degeneration of the forest has consequences for everyone.

We all see now that in many African countries there are terrible droughts and hunger, so I explain that that's because past generations did not think about today's generations: they forgot that their children, grandchildren and great-grandchildren were going to need nature, and they kept destroying the forests, and that's why things are the way they are now. Besides, the world needs the pure air we have here to breathe, so I tell them we have to take care of it. It's not just us, the whole world needs the Amazon.

But when someone is hungry and thinks that by burning he will get food, he doesn't usually worry about whether people in China or Italy will be able to breathe.

Well, before people didn't worry about it. They used to think, if I have something, what do I care about people who don't? But now there is a different vision in our region, because people here know that a lot of the work we're doing locally depends on money from other countries. So I tell them if others help us, we have to help them. We must stop thinking about ourselves all the time and understand that when we burn land a lot of carbon goes up into the atmosphere and ruins it. That's why the climate keeps getting stranger, and if it keeps going like this where will we end up?

Messias makes a living from his crops, his 470 beehives and his salary at the project. He still plays soccer every weekend and hates cities:

I can't stand the noise, the stress. I am calm here and I breathe good air. If I want to eat, I go fishing. I don't have to lock my door, I'm not afraid of being robbed. I only go to the city to learn things that I can bring back here, to my people.

In the meantime, he has had another son with the same woman, "his friend." Most women in the region give birth to many children, because no one ever talked to them about family planning:

It's a vicious cycle. To feed so many children with this slash-and-burn system, there is more deforestation, more destruction of nature. So the land stops producing food and, when these kids grow up, they will have nothing to eat. Family planning is very important to preserving nature.

Messias has recently been asked to run for councilman on the ruling Partido dos Trabalhadores ticket, and he doesn't know what to do. His politics are social, not partisan, he says, and he wants to keep it that way because party politics are full of dirty money, secret deals, pressure and corruption... But if he really wants to change things he might have to join a party, he says, and, for the first time in many years, he doesn't know what to do next.

FORESTS
THREATENED HOME TO INDIGENOUS PEOPLES

Between 2000 and 2005, the global annual loss of forest area was over 7 million hectares, or 0.18% of global forest area.[1] Globally, deforestation affects over one billion people, of which a majority live in developing countries.[2]

Rainforests in particular produce oxygen and store carbon, which mitigates the impact of carbon emissions on climate change.[3] Unfortunately, rainforests are also under threat from deforestation. In Amazonia, deforestation is projected to reduce precipitation, as about half of the precipitation is generated by the rainforest itself, through evapotranspiration from trees. The loss of precipitation risks being as high as 20%, leading to future dry periods, higher surface temperatures and change in forest structure.[4]

Deforestation is a contributing factor to climate change, and climate change in turn risk accelerating deforestation. While there are many efforts in place to halt the immediate loss of forests as a result of deforestation, the long-term effects of climate change on forest areas are becoming increasingly harder to avoid. As the global temperature warms up, forested ecosystems risk being displaced, as warmer temperatures will move climatic zones suitable for temperate and boreal plants. Evidence suggests that plant migration previously has taken place at a pace of 20-200 kilometres per century. Currently, the northward migration of climatic zones suitable for temperate and boreal plants risk being as much as 200-1,200 kilometres by the year 2100, meaning that plants risk lagging behind.[5]

Such changes have occurred all throughout the history of the Earth, but with global warming the speed dramatically increases, not allowing the soil and ecosystems to adapt the way they have historically.[6] In the eastern regions of Amazonia, increased temperature will most likely by the middle of the 21st century induce a decrease in soil water, which in turn will lead to tropical forest being gradually transformed into savannah.[7] For developing countries, mitigating the effects of climate change on deforested areas is greatly challenging, due to poverty and institutional constraints. In many countries, public, private and non-governmental actors find themselves lacking adequate resources to tackle the challenges, risking a continuing spiral of negative effects that will be even harder to counteract. Mechanisms that could provide financial incentives for alternatives to the clearing of forests are rarely in place.

Further to ecological shifts, deforestation and climate change also directly impact Indigenous Peoples, who inhabit rainforests all over the world. Indigenous Peoples face challenges not only in terms of effects such as extreme weather threatening crops and traditional lands, but also of political influence, as their forests gradually become more politicized through efforts to curb deforestation and climate change.

While the rights of Indigenous Peoples are increasingly recognized, most notably through the United Nations Declaration on the Rights of Indigenous Peoples, adopted in 2007, Indigenous Peoples are often ignored or systematically marginalized in decision-making related to their homeland forests.[8] Exclusion of Indigenous Peoples stem from both government institutions and programmes, as well as from the private sector, and risks leading to loss of traditional knowledge about forests.

Children and young people are particularly affected by deforestation, in short and long term. Deforestation and other unsustainable uses of forests increase the number of poor people, and the number of people who will face poverty in the future. This directly affects young people's choices; one example is threats to school enrolment.[9] As effects of climate change increase in strength, young Indigenous People living in rainforests will have to manage the response to tomorrow's challenges. In order to do be able to do this, they must be capacitated to be fully involved in work already being carried out. Hence, efforts to curb climate change and its effect on rainforests must include strategies to increase education enrolment and improve the livelihoods of young people.

Kilom

MARSHALLESE NOBLE
NOT LEAVING THE ISLAND

When Kilom was eight years old, he enjoyed listening to the stories that the old man would tell him in his cabin by the sea. In Majuro few houses are not by the sea: Majuro is an atoll, a coral island formed by a circle of narrow and spotty land around a lagoon. From coast to coast, the width of Majuro is usually no more than one hundred meters: it is 40 kilometres long but its surface area is not even 10 square kilometres.

Majuro is the capital of the Republic of the Marshall Islands, in Micronesia, thousands of kilometres away from any continent. The Republic consists of a group of 29 atolls that include more than 1200 islands and islets whose total area of solid ground is no more than 200 square kilometres. Only 70,000 people live in the Marshall Islands. A few years earlier, when Kilom was six years old and in first grade, he, like all the other children, had to march down the main – and only – street on the island with many others; flags were waving and music playing: that day, October 21,

1986, the Marshall Islands became independent, a republic in free association with the United States.

The old man would tell him stories about the islands, their myths and customs. One afternoon, the old man told Kilom that he, Kilom, may inherit all the land one day. He told him that he was an "allab", a noble, because his mother, Takbar, was a "le-iroij", a queen, and so he had to be all the more loyal to his land and respectful of its traditions. Kilom's father, Molik, was the son of a Japanese merchant who had come to the Islands in the 1920s – when Japan occupied them. After the defeat of Japan in 1945, Kilom's grandfather decided to go away for good. But in Marshallese culture, blood and possessions are passed on through the mother, and his mother was a "le-iroij". In Marshallese, that word means "everyone": the king or chieftain had to take responsibility for everyone else. Kilom found out that, centuries before, his mother's ancestors had come from an island, Mili, which still belongs to the family. They had conquered

lands in Majuro and in other islands in the archipelago. Kilom already loved his country but, from then on, he felt bound to it in on an almost supernatural level.

I feel so attached to this land. Land is very important to us, it is a precious gift. Our land is very limited, so we really have to take care of it, to fight for it.

Kilom grew up; life was quiet. In those years, there were fewer inhabitants and fewer houses on the Island. Kilom used to go to a beach directly in front of his house, where there is now a warehouse and a dock. During the week, Kilom went to school, played basketball or baseball, studied. On Saturdays and Sundays he would not only go to the church, but also fishing on neighbouring islands or hang out with friends, occasionally with a girl. But he had to be back home by 10 pm: the authority of the elders, at that time, was fairly strict.

With no computers and little television, the outside world was quite distant.

But there were, from time to time, jolts, like those days in 1990 when the Gulf War began and the Marshallese were frightened: their largest atoll, Kwajalein, is a major part of the US missile system and, for some weeks, they feared an attack.

Later on, Kilom came across other words that would mark his life. He was in his final years of elementary school when, for the first time, he heard the terms climate change and sea-level rise, but he didn't think they were important. Those foreigners who said that the Marshall Islands would sink into the sea must be joking. Years later, when

"I feel this place is part of me and I'm part of it. It's sad for me to imagine that, but it's going to happen: in the present situation there's not much we can do."

he was finishing high school and trying to decide what to study, he came across those terms again, but this time they did seem important. If it was true, as some believed, that the ocean was rising, his country would certainly end up disappearing. Kilom felt he

had to do something; to start, he decided to study marine biology.

I realized that the sea level rise was a matter of life and death for us: if the Island sinks, we just disappear as a country, as a people, as a culture.

One year later, when he was 20, Kilom found out that the Japanese government offered scholarships. He was interested; it was a good opportunity to learn new things and to find out about the other culture that he carried in his blood. He was selected; he travelled and studied civil engineering. Life in Tokyo was not easy; he had to learn the language and, moreover, how to live in a highly technological, work intense society, in a huge city where he had a 45-minute commute to the university every morning on a crowded train; in a country where there was such a thing as, for example, cold. But there were rewards; he saw snow for the first time; he learned a great deal, and he met Jane, a young Samoan woman also studying in Japan. When they graduated, Kilom and Jane went to Samoa, where they got married and had their first son. Six months after he was born, they were in Majuro.

When Kilom went back to the Islands, he had taken enough distance to recognize

the changes that his country and its culture had undergone in the previous decades: the most visible example was the food. For many years, the Marshallese just ate what they had: fish, shellfish, breadfruit, taro, coconut, sweet potato, banana, cassava, sugar cane, chicken, pigs. But from the Japanese they had gotten used to eating rice and noodles, and from the Americans bread, and now they had to import these things, and almost any other: foods, beverages, clothing, notebooks, safety pins, cars, detergents, televisions, dishware, medicines and, mostly, fuel for transportation and electricity.

Mostly, Kilom thinks, what changed the Marshallese culture was the advent of money: before, it did not exist on the Islands. People used to share what little they had – a fish, some vegetables, the labour required to build a house or a canoe – but then they grew greedier. He also noticed other problems:

The island has developed and that's good, but it wasn't properly planned, so now we are facing sanitary, environmental and health issues. The demographic growth has been very quick and the infrastructure can't handle it. But I'm still proud to be Marshallese. We are inventive people who

came to this island long ago and created new ways of living here. We are considered among the top navigators in the world; our people were able to sail hundreds of miles in their canoes, with no instruments whatsoever. We Marshallese are a part of this land and of this sea.

And Kilom became obsessed with his old issue: climate change and sea level rise. Kilom joined an NGO with whom he had worked, the Marshall Islands Conservation Society. So he started to address the issue full time:

Part of my work consists of advocating for protection of the reef and the marine resources we have. If we lose them we're doomed: we lose our source of revenue and the possibility of increasing tourism. But, most of all, when the reefs are healthy, they build up really fast, maybe faster than the sea level rises, so they could prolong our time above water.

Do you really think that the Islands might sink?

Well, until now the experts can't say how fast the sea-level is rising, so basically what we can do for the moment is help the reef grow healthier and faster to provide us with shelter from the waves, and more food. But I don't know... It's only small stuff that's not going to make any difference if the sea level increases rapidly.

One common way to stop the land from eroding is planting trees on the coast; in Majuro that is very difficult because on almost the entire shoreline there are houses and families, and not much room left for trees. Near the airport, the government has built a few seawalls to hold back the water, but they use limestone that, with dynamite, they blast out of the coral reef. As the struc-ture of the reefs is debilitated and reduced, the Island is further exposed to winds, storms and floods. In December 2008, for example, a surge in ocean waters flooded the Island. Thousands were forced to leave their homes and, on Christmas Day, the government declared a state of emergency. Now, scattered in the sand along the beach, are the gravestones of a cemetery that was washed away.

On the island, there are no construction materials, so if you want to reinforce one part of the island you have to sacrifice another.

Further, there are cement blocks called rib raps, which are strong and efficacious but expensive, and the government doesn't have money to buy them. In any case, these are temporary solutions that could work for just a few years.

I know there is going to be a time when this Island will be underwater. I don't know what's going to happen to our people, our way of life. There will no longer be a Marshallese language, a Marshallese culture, and for me that's really hard, because I feel so bound to this place. I love it and I consider it my own.

But you think it's inevitable?

It is inevitable. It is happening; the polar caps are melting rapidly and the sea level is rising accordingly. You can delay the process, but in the end we'll be underwater. Maybe in a hundred, maybe in two hundred years, who knows. But for me, if this happens in my lifetime, I'd rather die with this island than go elsewhere. I'll sink with the ship, because I feel this place is part of me and I'm part of it. It's sad for me to imagine that, but it's going to happen: in the present situation there's not much we can do. Imagine if your country was going to disappear under water.

The highest point in Majuro is three meters above sea level. Here, the threat is felt all the time.

What do you think about the people from other threatened islands who are looking for land elsewhere, like the Tuvalus or the Maldivians?

Well, there are even some Marshallese who would prefer to go to the United States. Not everyone's the same.

In the Marshall Islands there is a great deal of poverty and unemployment, and many young people don't think the way Kilom does; they prefer to get out while they can and – thanks to the free association – they have the right to live in the United States. In recent months, for instance, there was a program by which North American hotel companies hired 800 young people from Majuro to work at their establishments. In a population of 25,000, the sudden departure of 800 young people is a major blow.

But for me, this is the place where I'm going to die. My grandma, my great grandma, they are all buried here, so I'll be buried here too. I can't imagine living in another country for long. But it's hard to think that all the things you work for, you fight for, are going to disappear. Sometimes I ask myself, "Why am I doing this, why am I doing that?"

And what do you answer?

That it's better to do something, even in these conditions, than nothing at all. And, anyway, I'll do as much as I can to delay my land's sinking. At least, I will have tried, and that's my obligation.

SMALL ISLANDS
RISING SEAS AND CHOICES

While climate change is projected to affect all countries in some way, Small Island States face some of the greatest challenges. The people living in low-lying areas and smaller islands might indeed find their homes unliveable within the next century, due to rising sea-levels, tropical storms, and other climate change induced phenomena.[1] While facing these risks, many Small Island States are also developing countries with small populations, meaning that their abilities to prevent, mitigate and adapt to the projected climate change scenarios are severely hampered.

Rising sea-levels, which will partially or wholly cover Small Island States in the Pacific in water, has sprung up as one of the most frequently discussed climate change impacts. Some countries have already begun planning relocation of large portions of their populations, and as we see in Kilom's story, many who move away choose not to return.

Islands disappearing before the year 2100 are, however, not the only concern for people living in Small Island States. Already existing challenges are likely to be enhanced by climate change, and cause grave situations, before small islands become inhabitable due to rising sea-levels. Further, not all small islands are projected to be covered in water, but will face new challenges nonetheless. This means that long term solutions to the potential problems need to be developed, if Small Island States, that are not projected to disappear under rising seas, are to be inhabitable in the future.

One challenging issue shared by Small Island States across the world today relates to water supplies and access to freshwater. In general, access to water is scarce, and managing the limited supply is part of daily life. Projections are that climate change will further compromise the available water resources. This threat comes from rising sea-levels and changes in rainfall, which risk tainting the freshwater reserves with salt.[2] Some of these reductions may not be reversible.

Salinization also poses a threat to soil used to grow crops. In Micronesia, where Kilom lives, the staple food taro is grown in low-lying swamp areas, vulnerable to flooding by seawater containing dissolved salts. When the soil has been tainted by saltwater, cleaning the soil with normal rainfall takes up to two years, and the taro plant itself needs another two to three years before it is ready to harvest.[3] If saltwater intrusion through wave surges, rising sea-levels and precipitation occurs more frequently, the soil will have more difficulties recovering. Such loss of crops is a severe blow for economies of Small Islands States, many of which already rely heavily on food imports.

As many small islands lie in tropical or sub-tropical zones, diseases such as dengue, diarrhoea and malaria are a pressing concern for some Small Island States. While it is uncertain if, how and where climate change will lead to future increased disease incidence, this is an area of concern if temperatures rise, access to freshwater is compromised

and wet seasons change.[4] Other factors such as poor waste-management and lack of infrastructure also contribute to the spread of disease.

For small islands in higher latitudes, climate change is predicted to affect biological diversity. Iceland, a country partially dependent on its fishing industry for export incomes, will need to adapt to a possible collapse of the capelin stock, a forage fish preyed on by whales, seals and other predators that are part of the catch in the waters surrounding Iceland.[5]

Young people living in Small Island States face difficult decisions in the face of forthcoming climate change. Will they stay and do what they can as Kilom has decided to do, or will they leave to settle somewhere else? Regardless, climate change will likely have impacts on the lives of young people living on small islands, negatively affecting their livelihoods as well as their physical and psychological health. Whatever decisions young people living on Small Island States take regarding their future lives, we should ensure that the options are not hampered by lack of access to education, livelihoods and health services.

Mandisa

AMERICAN ORGANIZING FOR LIBERTY
RESPONDING TO A DISASTER

That Monday would change Mandisa's life, along with the lives of many others. In fact, the life of the entire city of New Orleans changed that Monday, August 29, 2005, when Hurricane Katrina hit town.

Mandisa was born in 1985 in Brooklyn, New York, where her parents had moved a dozen years earlier. Both were southerners: her mother was from South Carolina, her father from New Orleans. They had travelled up north looking for a better place to live: a place where being African American did not make things that much harder.

Historically, the South has always been lacking in resources and investment. At that time racism, although legally ended, was still alive around here. And New York was seen as the city where dreams could come true.

Mandisa's father was a doctor, the son of a dock worker and a hairdresser, who had received scholarships to study in California;

he practiced, at that time, in a New York hospital. Her mother was a community organizer fighting for women's rights. When Mandisa was six years old they decided to return to New Orleans, where their family and their roots were, to raise their kids – Mandisa has two older siblings – within their own culture. In New Orleans, culture is a very deep word: the city was Spanish and French before becoming the cradle of one of America's most important cultural forms, jazz music.

In New Orleans, Mandisa started school and she had to cope with some new problems: she was big, a stutterer and an African American, and for those reasons, some kids teased her.

I remember some kids saying 'you're dirty, you're dirty', so I went home crying and my mom wondered what's wrong and I said 'I want to take a shower, I'm dirty', and she said 'you're not dirty' and then she showed me pictures of my family: 'look, your dad's dark, your grandma, your uncles, we're all

dark, there is nothing dirty about you, this is the way we are and it's perfectly okay'.

Quite soon, Mandisa learned that people who consider themselves "normal" tend to despise "others," and she felt she had to stress her own position. In middle school, her group of friends consisted of seven or eight classmates whose identities were based on being different. Together they did anything that was out of fashion; they played chess, read sophisticated books, took French classes, played quiz contests, refused to go to the mall. They wanted to show the others that they were not like them.

Mandisa also attended a creative arts school where she got involved in the writing program; she was very busy, but that didn't stop her from spending a couple of hours a day in front of the TV set, or chatting with her friends through the Internet. When Mandisa was 16, she heard of a place where victims of domestic violence were given shelter, and that summer, Mandisa started to volunteer at the Crescent House, an institution where hundreds of abused women and their children are given support, temporary housing, education, legal advice. She couldn't stand the idea of a man beating his partner, and she had decided that she was going to be a family lawyer: that shelter was a good starting point.

Two years later, when it was time for her to go through that very American rite of passage, graduation and college visiting, Mandisa chose to stay in New Orleans, so she could continue with her work against domestic violence. Loyola University was a traditional Catholic institution, where she qualified for a scholarship.

"...it disrupted and changed my life. And I think it showed a lot of people that we don't have to rely on the government to save us, but to build social networks to save ourselves."

Anti-violence shaped my feminist identity, it's why I ended up with a minor in Women's Studies as an undergraduate. But I was also getting a very strong anti-racist identity, a pro-black identity. Racial profiling and discrimination were happening simultaneously.

In college, Mandisa met lots of new people: people from other states and countries. But she could not help feeling "othered" again: like that Parent's Day when she was told not to wear that t-shirt with the face of Angela Davis, the famous black activist, printed on it. Manisa started to get involved in campus politics, but she had to cope with the fact that the groups that opposed discrimination were scattered and, therefore, less effective. The groups dealing with gender or sexuality were not interested in issues of race, and vice versa. Mandisa tried to create bridges between the groups, and she grew too accustomed to hearing the same words time and again: "But that is not the real issue."

Though Mandisa moved to an apartment she shared with some classmates, she was growing weary of the college environment: she felt that, for too many, college life was about partying all the time, getting drunk and missing classes; it was not about taking any responsibility or trying to do any good in the world. So she began to withdraw from campus activism and go back to her community work. She took a class in Liberation Theology and, she says, it changed her life: she understood that she thought of her political work in terms of "helping people," rather than justice and

liberation. She realized that, by trying to "help" poor people she was "othering" them the same way people had "othered" her.

A few weeks later, in spring of 2005, Mandisa attended a conference held by a group called Insight about Women of Colour against Violence. There, she felt she had found a space that could address her questions not one by one but all together. This group was able and willing to relate issues of gender, race, class, violence and sex in order to understand the whole picture.

And then came that Monday. Hurricanes have always existed, but many scientists think that their strength and frequency are on the rise because of climate change: what used to be a very unusual occurrence is going to become more and more frequent. Hurricane Katrina was a moderate Category 1 storm when it crossed southern Florida, but it gained force while crossing the Gulf of Mexico because of what scientists call a "diminished braking mechanism": if a cyclone finds in its path colder water, its intensity weakens. Katrina, on the contrary, was intensified by the warm water in the Gulf of Mexico. By the time it arrived to southeast Louisiana on Monday morning, Hurricane Katrina was a Category 3 storm that broke through New Orleans's

estimated in excess of 100 billion U.S. dollars. Thousands and thousands lost their houses; in those first days, a great number of the city's inhabitants did not have anywhere to go home to. To this day, many haven't been able to return.

In Mandisa's eyes, the whole thing was a mess. Far from everyone had the capacity to leave the city when the evacuation order came, and as with most natural disasters, things weren't making sense. Mandisa was furious:

How was it possible that reporters could get into the city to take pictures of people dying yet people couldn't get out? I couldn't fathom it. I couldn't understand how animals in the zoo could be evacuated before people.

When Mandisa came back to New Orleans, her question was "How do I live with what I want do in this world?" And her first answer was to get involved in the housing issue, to work to bring back the displaced people to suitable places. Mandisa would spend days listening to victims of the Hurricane, who were waiting to be forced to leave their shelters at any minute. Many other problems emerged as well; people were out of work, as the Hurricane had destroyed

protection system at fifty points, flooding more than three quarters of the city.

Earlier in the summer, Mandisa had started to work as a bartender in the French Quarter. That Saturday, Mandisa had worked until 9 am; she was very tired when her mother called her to say that a hurricane was coming and she had to leave town; the whole family was going to an aunt's house in Atlanta. She said she wouldn't go; she had already made plans for the day. Her parents did not give up; in the end, on Sunday morning, her older brother came by her apartment to pack her stuff and take her with them to Atlanta.

The images on TV that Monday were not so dramatic, and Mandisa thought it hadn't been that bad after all. But in the evening she got text messages from her friends saying that the levees were breaking and the city was full of water. The TV started to show it too, and she began to understand that something terrible was happening. The next day, a roommate of Mandisa's told her that their apartment was under six feet of water and they had lost everything in it; then she learned that the community centre she worked at was completely flooded, and the university was not going to open for some months. Little by little, she came to realize that her city was never going to be the same.

Hurricane Katrina killed at least 1,836 people, and was qualified as "the largest natural disaster in the history of the United States." Economic damage is their workplace, and the service industry suffered greatly from the halt in tourism. There was also social unrest. Mandisa had lost everything she had, and she started to drink, as a way to cope with so much loss, and to create a space in which to talk with friends about their experiences of the Hurricane:

After Katrina many people had mental health related needs, like counselling and therapy, but it was difficult to access. And as one of my friends always says, 'A Mad Dog only costs one dollar and forty-nine cents'.

In her work, Mandisa noticed that in this natural disaster as in many others, women tended to bear the brunt of the burden. They are the most vulnerable heads of households; they have to take care of the children; they risk being victims of sexual violence; and they might not be able to access the specific health care they need. Through a woman she had met at the Insight Conference, she contacted the Women's Health and Justice Initiative and in 2006 became part of a group that decided to establish a specialized women's health clinic.

We wanted a place where women can access free or low cost quality, affordable, holistic health care, in an environment that was not judgmental, and acknowledged that people are dealing with multiple personal problems, post Katrina.

For Mandisa it was important to engage in addressing the root causes of why women have health concerns, and what that means in a situation following a natural disaster. After a lot of volunteering and fundraising, the clinic opened in May 2007. At the same time, Mandisa received a grant from a foundation that allowed her to give up bartending and work full time as a community organizer, with both the Women's Health Initiative and another group called the Institute of Women and Ethnic Studies, on a HIV and AIDS project where she would become a sexual health educator.

Mandisa had already finished college, in a rush: she did not feel any need to do it at the time, but she did not want to lose her previous efforts, and graduated in History, Sociology, Political Science, and Women's Studies.

How would you define yourself?

As someone who is working for liberation. Or as an organizer. I guess I'm undecided as to what term I'd use. But now everything's changing a little bit, because I have enrolled in law school for next year, at Louisiana State University, which is like an hour from here.

Mandisa doesn't want to be a lawyer, she says, but rather to acquire the legal skills that she will need for her social and political work. So she will leave the city where she has always lived, and her activities, to get new tools that will allow her to continue organizing.

Katrina played a major part in all this. For me it was a tremendous shock; it disrupted and changed my life. And I think it showed a lot of people that we don't have to rely on the government to save us, but to build social networks to save ourselves.

NATURAL DISASTERS
WOMEN IN THE EYE OF THE STORM

Hurricanes, such as Katrina in 2005, are striking examples of extreme weather phenomena that claim a high human toll, destroy infrastructure, cause psychological suffering and burden governments and cities with heavy financial implications. As the climate changes and temperatures rise, disasters induced by weather are likely to become more common, and more severe. Projections of such an increased impact are difficult, but one attempt has been made by the Global Humanitarian Forum, predicting that in 2030, the number of weather-related disasters globally will multiply, compared to the period 1975-2008.[1]

Currently, coastal cities in both developed and developing countries are growing and expanding, due to rural-to-urban migration and natural population growth within cities. Such urban growth sometimes leads to loss of wetlands in river deltas, which is problematic because wetlands have the ability to buff the effects of storms and floods. The same applies to forests, with one example being the flood damage in Central America after Hurricane Mitch in 1998, which was more severe than it would have been without deforestation in the region.[2] Cities in other locations sensitive to dramatic weather events, such as inland ravines and slopes, are also growing, meaning that people living in such inland cities can expect similar challenges.

The impacts of natural disasters are both immediate and long term. Death or injuries through drowning, electrocution or asphyxiation are the most immediate effects. In the first months after water related disasters such as a hurricane or flood, the risk of outbreaks of water-borne and vector-borne diseases increases. The risk increases if there are significant population displacements. However, with the appropriate strategies, major disease outbreaks are usually prevented. [3,4] The challenge for developing countries lies in adapting to more frequent risks, which requires infrastructure and funding, straining already strained economies.

The long term effects of natural disasters are manifold, and vary between different disasters, based on factors such as the type of disaster, the effectiveness of emergency response and the number of people affected. Generally, there are risks for social unrest, trauma and disruption of the rule of law. Mental health aspects of post-disaster situations might not be as visible as physical injury or damage to infrastructure, but are nonetheless a great part of the impact. Behaviours of people in post-disaster areas may change, including more risk-taking and activities that might be harmful to oneself (such as excessive consumption of alcohol) or others (such as violence).

With regards to reproductive health, disasters and crisis situations are a serious concern. Typically, when people are displaced due to a crisis, the percentage of pregnant women who suffer life-threatening complications is on par with pregnant women in general, but the access to emergency obstetric care might be seriously hampered. Distribution of reproductive health commodities such as medication and contraceptives risks being temporarily reduced. If people are displaced for longer periods, living in camps or temporary homes, problems such as domestic violence and rape are likely to increase.[5]

Overall, women are more vulnerable to the impact of disasters than men, due to their subordinate position in male-dominated societies. Moreover, during a crisis, gender-based inequalities are often enhanced. Carrying out household chores risks being more difficult in a crisis context in which access to fuel, water and food is scarce. Further, perceiving men as the breadwinner of a family, disaster relief authorities and organizations might turn to them in order to reach families, leaving women and their specific concerns in the shadows, especially those of single-female headed households. Women's economic recovery after a disaster often takes longer compared to men's economic recovery, due to the precariousness of the socio-economic status of women.[6]

With regards to young people, disasters risk depriving them of education, health services and social networks, increasing the risks of engaging in hazardous practices. Efforts to mitigate the effects (short term and long term) of disasters must therefore take into account, among many other factors, that young people are sexually active, and that the risk of unwanted pregnancies and sexually transmitted infections might increase if access to reproductive health services are disrupted.

Youness

MOROCCAN FOOTBALLER
ADAPTING TO A NEW LIFE

At first, he thought that it was a rain just like so many others, but it had already lasted four days. That morning in February of 2009, Youness was chatting and playing cards with his friends in their usual meeting place, a ruined house on a hill at the entrance to his town. His town was a tiny valley with two dozen houses on the outskirts of Slimane, a city of 150,000 in the centre of Morocco. Not far from the capital Rabat, this is a region of gentle hills and mild temperatures suited to agriculture. Youness is not a farmer, but his father is. Twenty years ago, his parents came to this region from the south, near Marrakech, looking for a better place to raise crops and live. The south is hot and dry; on the plains of Gharb, near Sidi Slimane, the climate is milder and humid, and the soil more fertile. Here, they were able to buy two hectares of land and they began to grow bananas and strawberries.

Suddenly that morning, in the middle of their games, Youness and his friends heard something strange: shouting, sudden movements. So they walked out of the ruined house to see what was going on; they saw their neighbours shouting and running about because their houses were flooding. The houses were made from mud bricks; in the valley, the water already came up to people's waists, and everyone was struggling to salvage their mattresses, furniture and clothing. Youness and his friends ran down and started looking for buckets to help out.

By around three in the afternoon, things seemed under control: the houses that were most affected had been evacuated and the rain was slowing down. The neighbours were tired and annoyed, but a bit calmer. In the end, it wasn't any worse than things they had experienced before.

That night at dinner, Youness and his parents talked about what had happened that day. They talked about whether Mohammed had lost his radio or Hanae been left without clothes for her baby. At least the rain had stopped, they said, and the water had not reached their house, which was on slightly higher ground. At around nine, Youness was watching television when a deluge began drumming on the roof. At eleven it was still raining just as hard, and Youness heard shouting and a sound that he had never heard before: a sort of tatatata. Later he would describe it similar to an enormous animal stampeding. Youness walked outside; in the darkness, he could perceive that the houses below were sinking. The river had overflowed and there was water everywhere. The shouts, in the middle of the night, were terrifying.

Youness went inside to fetch his parents and his brother. Just barely dressed and without taking anything with them, they left home and ran to the top of the hill. Shouting for help, others did the same. Everyone was frightened and soaking wet;

freezing, they tried to take shelter under a tree but the water still made its way to them. They kept hearing noises, shouting; they couldn't tell because it was so dark, but they supposed that these were the sounds of children running, of parents trying to get them out, of attempts to salvage something as they fled. In a few minutes, there were twenty or thirty people under the trees; in hushed tones, as if their anxiety forced them to talk quietly, they tried to understand what was going on.

"I always liked the idea of being the one to teach, organize, run things... I like being able to tell others what I know."

What were you thinking about when you were there?

About death, just death. I had never experienced anything like it. I thought that no one would be able to help us, that the water level would keep rising and, in the end, would cover us all and kill us.

Almost everyone cried and prayed. Youness asked his God to get him out alive. But he kept hearing the noises and the shouts, and he thought that he had to do something. Two or three men went towards the flood, and Youness decided to go along:

I am going down there to help out.

Please, son, don't go. Don't do it. Please don't.

Youness tried to explain to his mother that he had to go; his mother was crying and telling him not to, that if he did he would not make it back, that he would die down there. She said that if he went down to help out she would die of a heart attack. Youness stayed where he was; later, that decision would weigh on his soul.

Youness had been born twenty-two years earlier; his childhood was peaceful. He played football with the kids from his town, swam in the river, talked with them about what they would do when they grew up. Youness was good at football and a serious fan of Real Madrid: he used to say that one day he would play, inshAllah, on that team. But he also liked to read and study, and he easily finished grade school. He went on to high school, and when he was twenty

he graduated; the next year, his parents were able to send him to Mohammed V University in Rabat, where Youness wanted to pursue English Studies. But he couldn't; there were no openings in that department, so Youness signed up for French Studies. He was not as successful in this field – 'I didn't like French, and the grammar is so complicated' – and the next year he went back to his town. There, Youness began working every afternoon in a small internet café, and he signed up for a two-year program in clothing design. He thought that, when he was older, he would be able to design jeans, and hence get a job in a big city and "lead a good life." Many of his neighbours had already left because the land had become much less productive due to soil exhaustion. They had migrated to large cities or left the country altogether.

What does "leading a good life" mean?

Having a job, a house, a car and a wonderful woman. That's a good life.

Until that night when the water came and took everything away. Under the trees, Youness saw – or, rather, heard – how the houses below collapsed under the weight of the water. Youness was convinced that none of this was really happening, that he was having a nightmare. And he couldn't wake up.

At four in the morning, they heard the sound of some engines; it was the first aid. People from the region who came in small zodiac-type boats or canoes to try to help out. Near dawn the rain stopped; a few hours later, Youness and his parents were able to go back to their house, which was now a ruin full of mud and stones; the furniture, clothing and other objects had been destroyed by the water. They tried to clear a space to rest but they couldn't. Little by little, Youness understood that they no longer had a house and, from that moment on, his life would never be the same.

But the worst was still to come: a little later, Youness learned that Ali, his best friend, had died along with his whole family when the roof to their house collapsed.

I still think about that night all the time. I can't get it out of my mind; it still pains me.

What exactly do you think of?

I blame myself. I do, because I didn't do anything for other people, I wasn't able to help them. Especially my friend, who was so close to me, and I didn't do anything for him…

Why couldn't you help him?

I already told you, I was afraid of death. I didn't want to worry my mother… I don't know, I should have done more to help the others, something more than just looking on.

At around ten in the morning the water began to recede: everything was covered with mud, trash, chunks of things, dead animals. The public aid services arrived at around midday, too late to save many lives. All they could do was to remove the ruins, recover the bodies. That afternoon, Youness and his family tried to rest in a makeshift refuge of blankets and sheets of plastic; Youness was exhausted but he could not stop thinking about his dead friend, lost house, ruined fields and vanished future.

Why do you think all that happened?

Because of the weather, which has changed so much as a result of globalization. There are too many cars, buses, people, industries, and so the climates is changing and things like this happen: I have lost my home, my land, my friends …

That night other aid groups arrived with tents and food. Among them was Naciri, the President of the Association de Soutien aux Espaces Santé Jeunes. A young man of 24 who lives in Rabat, Naciri had received, early that morning, a request for help from local members of the Association. In a few hours, some forty volunteers from this peer's educators net had moved into the area:

When we arrived, we couldn't believe what we saw: everything was covered with water. The first thing we did was go through the region in some boats that belonged to the Civil Protection Service to try to save the desperate people who were still trapped on the roofs of their houses.

That same morning they found the head of the local chapter of the Association. He had gotten trapped while trying to save a man who was sinking in the mud. Those mud holes posed the greatest danger; they were covered by a superficial layer of water and, if someone stepped on them without realizing it, they could get trapped for good. Naciri tried to get the two men out but he couldn't; after a few endless moments pulling on ropes, they were finally able to get them out. Two hours later, when they took Naciri's friend back to the town, he learned that his mother and sister had drowned.

But the worst thing happened the second day, when we came across a family that was holding out on top of the roof of a house. They saw us and started to call for help. We were on our way to them when we received a warning through the radio. We were told that a second wave of water was about to set in and that we should leave. We tried to make it over to help them, but we saw the water coming and had to move back.

Did you agree with the decision to withdrawal?

We had no choice. If we stayed, we would have died as well. But it was awful. I was left with such a feeling of sadness. I couldn't sleep for a long time.

The young people from the Association worked ceaselessly for three days and three nights, and that was when Youness met them. Days later, when Youness's father decided to take the whole family to the house of his oldest son, in Rabat, they helped them. Youness's family was not the only one to leave everything behind. In the region there are a many ruined houses, streets and schools, and it will take a great deal of effort to make the land productive again. The figures are not exact, but an estimated 40 percent of the region's inhabitants have not yet returned – and many have no intention of doing so.

Are you going to go back to your town?

No, never.

Why not?

For many reasons. I am trying to forget about all that and think about my future. I don't think that any of us will return. We no longer have anything there, and we don't want to do anything there either. My best friend died, so why go back? I prefer to think about the time we spent together…

Now, thanks to the ASESJ, Youness is taking a six-month course to learn to take calls at a call centre. In the meantime, he is doing construction work; his job consists of carrying buckets and stones and bricks about, and they pay him 50 dirhams – about 6 US dollars – for a seven- or eight-hour workday.

This is not what I should be doing. I have a degree; this is not a real job.

He says, almost ashamed.

It's just that for now I have to do this to get by and help my family, to forget about all that and start to live again.

Youness is sad and confused. He thinks that he might be able to go to England, which has always attracted him. He believes it has a lot to offer people who want to live there; he says, for instance, that if you have a diploma you can get a job easily. Meanwhile, he is still taking courses and working, and trying to have some good moments. He has a girlfriend, but he says that, at least for now, it's nothing serious, just someone with whom to talk and have fun.

You know, teenagers…

But you're 22.

Youness laughs for the first time and acknowledges:

It's true, I am 22. I had better get on with it if I want to have a future.

MIGRATION
RISING TEMPERATURE AND MOVING POPULATIONS

As early as 1990, the Intergovernmental Panel on Climate Change stated that the most severe impact on populations from climate change may be the displacement of people.[1] The report talked about "millions" of people. Today, migration remains one of the key issues when discussing climate change impact, but estimates are very difficult to make, due to lack of data and the complexity of migration issues, in particular with regards to the differentiation between voluntary and forced migration. The International Organization for Migration (IOM) has pointed out that projections of people on the move due to climate change vary between 25 million and 1 billion.[2] The rather large differences in projections depend on which of the scenarios of the Intergovernmental Panel on Climate Change one chooses as base, as well as which definition of "migration" is used. It is however clear that we can expect a significant increase in the movement of people because of climate change.

There are mainly two environmental push elements that can lead to migration: Sudden onset events with a direct impact, such as hurricanes, floods or droughts, and slow onset events, that is to say the progressive evolution of the environment, such as raising sea-levels.[3] While not all environmental change can be clearly linked to climate change, climate change is predicted to increase the force and frequency of the two push elements. As these two types of causes for migration could almost be considered dichotomies, the characteristics, responses and therefore consequences differ greatly.

Hurricanes and floods are events that are easy to identify when they occur, and to some extent we can also predict where they are likely to occur. With that knowledge, mitigation as well as early adaptation strategies can be put in place. On the other hand, there is no way of predicting how climate change will affect when or where natural disasters will occur in the coming century. Under unfortunate circumstances, the impact might be dire and large populations risk being temporarily displaced from their homes, perhaps not being able to return for many years.

While many of the populations who are more likely to be forced to migrate because of climate change live in developing countries, the poorest and most vulnerable are not necessarily the most likely to migrate. Migration as an adaptation strategy is very costly. One typically must have access to financial capital and social network in the place of destination. Furthermore, migration disrupts cultural and political life. Migration caused by climate change will hence not only depend on actual climate change, but also on economic, cultural, political and social factors.[4]

This means that responses to climate change induced movement of people must take more factors into account. For example, a gender perspective is essential; both if the migration is temporary or permanent. Displaced women are more vulnerable than men, as women often have a lower status than men and can expect their needs to be less attended to.

When a new life has to be formed after permanently migrating, the socio-economic status of migrant women may be affected by the fact that migrant women more often end up in the informal employment sector or having to carry out domestic work; in particular under precarious working conditions. Migrant women risk health concerns relating to potential difficulties in accessing social services in general and reproductive health services in particular, due to language barriers and legal and/or financial fences. Security is also an issue, as migrant women are more likely to be victims of domestic violence and abuse.[5]

While there are challenges, one must also remember that migration will, for some populations, be a necessary way of adapting to climate change in the coming century. Migration as adaptation strategy has indeed been present all through human history. It is therefore crucial to give attention to concerns for migrant populations, including migrant women and youth, both before, during and after moving.

Fatima

NIGERIAN ACTIVIST AND ORGANIZER
REPLACING FIREWOOD WITH A CELL PHONE

Fatima never wanted to be where she was. When she would see her older brothers and sisters leave for school, she would cry because she couldn't go with them. But when they started taking her to school, she would cry because she didn't want to stay by herself. Fatima has always had the feeling that things were never just as they should be, that she had to keep looking for something else.

Fatima was born in 1986 in Jos, a city with half a million inhabitants in the centre of Nigeria. Her father, Abubakar, had a management position at a mining corporation; he owned his own house and car, and was able to support the ten children he had with Aisha, a pious and devoted woman who spent what little free time she had knitting and spinning thread to help make ends meet.

When she was a child, Fatima was surrounded by brothers and sisters, and her life was almost easy. She had to walk for an hour to get to and from school, but when she got home there always was something good to eat, and she would take a nap before helping with the house chores and, every other day, washing her uniform. Fatima and her siblings had to see to their responsibilities before going outside to play.

Fatima belongs to a small tribe, the Egbira. Once a year, her family travels to "its" town; though none of them had been born in Toto, their grandparents were from there. It was a peaceful place where they would get in touch with their heritage. It was there that Fatima learned, for example, to respect her elders: that one must not only bow, but also kneel before them. Fatima did it, but she wondered why. Fatima was always challenging the reasons for everything. She wondered, for example, why she never saw a woman driving a car or, later, why all the people on TV and the radio defending women's rights were men. At home, Fatima had often heard the African saying that goes, "He who wears the shoe knows where it pinches most,"

but for some reason that didn't seem to apply to women.

Fatima was particularly interested in one of those television programs, aired on a local channel, it was called Youth Perspectives and its host was Mr. Kingsley Bangwell. He spoke of health issues, HIV, the environment, youth participation, entrepreneurship. Fatima hoped that one day she would go and see him and so, when Kingsley went to her school and asked people to help out in the community, she thought it was a sign. The next day, Fatima – now 16 – became a volunteer with the Young Stars Foundation.

It was mind blowing. There were so many resources to read from, so many interesting things to learn. I began to get into youth participation, governance issues, economic empowerment, sustainable development.

Young Stars Foundation was where Fatima saw a computer for the first time. They taught her what it was for. They also taught her how to make cosmetics, soap and candles and how to dye clothing, so to be able to train unemployed youth. At first, she didn't have a lot of self-confidence, but gradually she came to trust herself more. She loved feeling that she was doing something that mattered: she was no longer an observer, but a player. Until something unexpected happened that changed her life: her mother had a stroke and was paralyzed. A few months later, a second stroke killed her.

"... I didn't even know that I was causing harm to myself and to the rest of the world, both by cutting down trees and by the CO_2 emissions."

I always loved being a child. You're so innocent, and everything comes so easy. But when my mother died, a huge feeling of responsibility fell on my shoulders, because automatically I had to start taking care of my siblings: that's when I knew that I was not a child anymore.

She felt that her world had crumbled and wondered why to go on. It comforted her to think that her mother had had a good life, and that if her Creator took her, He must have had his reasons. When she felt ready, she wrote an article about her mother, entitled *Never Give Up*. That was the lesson that Fatima had learned from her mother's life, and it was the first time she wrote something with the idea of publishing it; those who read it liked it, and encouraged Fatima to keep on. Fatima thought about writing a novel that would tell the real life stories of girls like her. And so she started working on *The Face of Africa*, which she intends to finish soon, and then *The Amazon of Elkira*. She also changed her mind about becoming a doctor, the profession that she had always wanted to pursue; she would never be able to look at a sick person again without thinking of her mother.

Fatima had finished high school but she didn't go to the university because her family couldn't afford tuition. She kept doing community work, and that's how she came into contact with the people from the British Council. A few months later, she was selected to participate in Global Exchange, a program for young people from Nigeria and England. Thanks to the program, she would spend three months in Birmingham, England.

It was my first time so far from home, I was homesick. Everything was so different there. For one thing, I was surprised by how neat and punctual everything was, from meetings to buses.

But she found the food flavourless and, mostly, she was shocked to see young people drinking and smoking in the streets, dressed without any modesty and treating elders as if they were their equals. Fatima began to appreciate her own country more. It may be poor, she thought, but it has values that shouldn't be thrown away. She was very busy; she worked with women at a homeless shelter and on HIV and AIDS prevention campaigns. She learned that even a rich country like England was not a bed of roses for everyone.

Back in Jos, she started working with Spring of Life – an NGO focused on HIV and AIDS issues – trying to support patients not to give up, and to explain to them that, if they take good care of themselves, they can live with their disease for many years. She eventually started working as a volunteer at YARAC – Youth Adolescent Reflection and Action Centre – an NGO that, from the very beginning, allowed her to work on her own project, Young Women of Vision. There, she worked – and still works – organizing workshops on a variety of issues: the first one was on reproductive health and the prevention of STDs.

Very few Muslim girls from here would do what I'm doing. Women here are much more passive. It's in our culture; we are supposed to be housewives and that's all. But that's why so much work needs to be done.

Fatima was 19 and didn't plan to study, because she was already doing what she wanted to do and so it seemed like a waste of time. Then she realized that she needed to: "It's not just about wanting to change lives; it's about knowing how to change them," she realized. "And for that I needed a university education."

Even though she didn't have any money, she applied; when she was accepted, YARAC lent her what she needed. Due to her work in the community, she decided to study psychology. She is now in her third year, and she still works with YARAC, and with Action Aid on anti-hunger and food-rights campaigns. She is working on six or seven other projects as well and she doesn't have time – she has never had time – for a boy-friend. But last year, when she first heard about climate change at a meeting of Global

Exchange vets, she felt that she had to do something.

It was a revelation. I use firewood to cook, and I didn't even know that I was causing harm to myself and to the rest of the world, both by cutting down trees and by the CO_2 emissions. I used to throw cans and bottles anywhere, and they'll outlive us, they'll harm future generations.

Fatima still cooks with firewood because she has no choice, but soon she will get a special stove, crafted by an environmental-ist organization, that consumes less and produces fewer emissions. She also got

interested in the problem of water in her city, which affects her directly. Ten years ago, her house and the whole neighbour-hood stopped having tap water, and later her well ran out of water and they had to build another one, that doesn't provide drinking water. She is not the only one; due to a lack of infrastructure, most Africans have always had serious problems getting water; this problem has worsened in recent years with the indiscriminate chopping down of trees and the droughts associated with climate change.

Fatima started to think a lot about the issue, and she learned about a WaterAid program that offered a thousand US dollars to young people who wanted to use new technologies to carry on a project on water and sanitation. But, at 22, Fatima was too old to apply, so her 17-year-old sister, Amina, joined in and they presented an idea; they would put together a group of young people from different communities to film on their cell phones – in Nigeria, where landlines never worked, almost all urban dwellers have cell phones – the problems caused by the lack or misuse of water and of the sanitation system. They would edit a 15-minute documentary to be shown and discussed at schools, and then put together groups to work on the issue and demand action from the local government. The proposal was accepted and they will soon start working.

Why water?

Because I have not had running water for ten years, because everyone complains about this, because the lack of water is disastrous on all fronts: families cannot cook healthy food, live healthy lives, or maintain vegetable gardens and animals. And women have to walk and walk to get water. If a girl does not have water she cannot wash her uniform and so she cannot go to school, because people laugh at you if your uniform is dirty. We need water all the time. It's so important and, sometimes, so neglected.

Why do you feel the need to do these things all the time?

At first it was out of curiosity: I wanted to know. Now it is more the satisfaction of doing something that is beneficial. And it's exciting to meet so many people, and it builds my CV, of course, says Fatima, laughingly.

The most important thing, she says, is that you never know whose life will be changed by the small things you do. That is what makes her keep going, and she talks about more and more project; she can't stop thinking up projects and imagining the future.

So, how do you see yourself in twenty years?

A psychologist, a wife, a very good mother, a writer hopefully, a development worker for sure. I might even be an entrepreneur producing cosmetics… I should be able to do a lot more than I'm doing now. I know that now I'm doing all I can to change lives, and I imagine that in twenty years I'll be doing the same thing but on a larger scale. I hate seeing people suffer from lacks: lack of food, of health care, of education, of water. They should have all these things.

And she tells the story of a woman from a nearby town who could not take her child to the doctor because the drought had ruined the crops and so she did not have the 20 US cents to pay for a motorcycle taxi. When she managed to get the money together and take him to the doctor, he was dying; the mother came home again carrying his body in her arms.

This is happening in 2009, in our cities. Why would a child die for not having access to health care and food and clean water? What will we do? What are we doing now?

POVERTY
CLIMATE CHANGE AND THE MILLENNIUM DEVELOPMENT GOALS

The impact of climate change will be most severe on the lives of poor people. While climate change impacts will wary geographically, poor people will be more vulnerable in impacted places, as poor people have less access to key economic and social capital, such as education, private savings, and mobility, all needed in adaptation to projected impact and change.

The effects on the lives of poor people, and the level of resilience to projected changes, naturally varies to a large extent – there will be as many altered lives as there are people living in poverty in places where climate change impact will occur. In cities, poor people will be more vulnerable to health problems induced by increased heat waves and reduced urban air quality, as well as to transmissible diseases including malaria, dengue and cholera, and rodent borne infections following floods or droughts.[1] In rural areas, small-scale agriculture and fishing is threatened by projected changes in precipitation, dry and wet seasons and temperature. Poor urban workers, typically employed in the informal sector, will be vulnerable to warmer temperatures and heat waves, as they often spend long hours in facilities without adequate ventilation and sanitation. Poor people displaced by climate change impacts, often moving to urban areas, might face difficulties in finding work.

Most developing countries have less capacity to allocate capital and human resources needed to respond proactively to climate change, compared to developed countries. The most vulnerable countries are located in tropical and sub-tropical areas, meaning that some of the most severe projected impact will target the countries that are least prepared.[2] However, societies and communities with high capacity are also vulnerable.[3]

Among the poor, women are expected to face harder consequences compared to men, because of their comparatively lower socio-economic status and women's high dependency on natural resources for their livelihoods. This applies is particular to single female headed households with few assets.[4] Two-thirds of the poor in world are women, and about 70-80 percent of agricultural workers are women. Further, as women spend less time in public spaces, they don't have the same preparation, as men, needed to cope with sudden disasters, with the effect that in many cases, a disproportionate number of women die or suffer injury.[5] Hence, adaptation and mitigation strategies must include special attention to women and girls, and their empowerment, which is partly dependent on their access to reproductive health.

With the global population being compromised by a large generation under the age of 25, young people will not only need to prepare to tackle tomorrow's impacts, but also be involved today in order to prepare themselves and their communities. Young poor people often have insufficient access to education, food, health, including reproductive health, and stable social networks such as their immediate family, thus making them more vulnerable. Today's young generation is also more urbanized than ever before, and in many cities, young people compromise a disproportionate number of slum dwellers.[6] With adequate efforts, urban young people have the potential to be strong actors in adaptation and mitigation, as cities provide opportunities both in terms of livelihoods and environmentally sound living. However, this requires that special attention be given to urban young people's needs.

As long as the global community fails in keeping the necessary pace with agreed development plans, such as the Millennium Development Goals (MDGs), climate change impacts for developing countries and poor people risk being more severe than they need be, as poverty exacerbates people's and countries' vulnerability to climate change.[7] Further, if we fail to adapt to and mitigate the effects of climate change, poverty risks increasing in already poor countries, which in the long run will, among other effects, add to a decrease in social services, especially basic health services, including reproductive health, and a loss of progress made in efforts to achieve universal access to sexual and reproductive health, the second target to be achieved under MDG 5 on maternal health. Currently, there is indeed risk that some of the headway made in the efforts to reach the MDGs will diminish because of climate change.[8]

At the Frontier: Young People and Climate Change

The seven stories in this report are all very real illustrations of what is likely to happen to millions of young people within the coming decades, if the impact of climate change is not subdued, and if the roots of climate change are not addressed. The effects will most likely be worst for young people living in poverty, and it is the level of attention we give to the needs of young people who are standing at the frontier of climate change, which determines how their lives will evolve.

The in-depth accounts of Marjorie, Mariama, Messias, Kilom, Mandisa, Youness and Fatima are examples of how young people's thoughts, dreams and actions are affected by climate change. Indeed, young people all over the world are engaging in climate change, from the deep forests in the Amazonia, the arid regions of Niger, the atolls and islands of the Pacific to the high-level discussions in the run-up to the United Nations Climate Change Conference in Copenhagen, in December 2009. As young people are lifting the challenges of climate change onto their shoulders, there is a great need for support to young people, strengthening them in their strive to safeguard the richness and diversity of the Earth for themselves and the generations to come.

As the people most vulnerable to climate change live in developing countries, poverty perspectives are key, when aiming at equipping young people with tools to adapt to and mitigate the effects of climate change. Thus, reducing poverty and improving the health of young people will reduce young people's vulnerability to climate change. Education, employment opportunities, access to health services including reproductive health and freedom from harm are all prerequisites if today's generation of young

"Young people must be able to take advantage of the progress that has been made in the direction of more climate friendly ways of life, supported by the advancement of technology."

people are to be ready for the future. This is particularly important for young people in towns and cities, as an increasing amount of the global population is concentrated in urban areas.

While reducing poverty is key, growth and the creation of wealth must materialize in new ways. Development cannot come at a cost of ever increasing greenhouse gas emissions, and developed countries cannot remain at the same emission levels as today. If we continue to produce climate change through patterns of production and consumption that create the same or higher emissions, we risk crossing the tipping point of natural and human mitigation capacities. Fortunately, other ways of living exist, and where they exist, they work. Young people must be able to take advantage of the progress that has been made in the direction of more climate friendly ways of life, supported by the advancement of technology.

Governments, policy makers, researchers, donors and international organizations have to recognize that young people are to be given a crucial role in adaptation to and mitigation of climate change. Governments and policy makers should promote the involvement of young people on all levels of discussions related to adaptation and mitigation, as young people will implement what is decided today, and live with the consequences. Researchers should create more data and analysis on how young people are affected and what the best responses are, as most impact scenarios omit specific analysis on young people.

Donors need to recognize that a larger youth generation than ever before lives in the world, and take steps to exploit their potential as agents for change. International organizations should advocate strongly for the empowerment of young people at all levels of climate change policies and programmes. Young people should establish networks and organize in taking on the challenge of climate change. If the key development actors support young people in the ways suggested, young people themselves will be better prepared to play their part and engage in the response to climate change, today and tomorrow. We must strengthen young people's commitment to the demanding task of climate change. If we adults don't, then it is to our collective peril.

Endnotes

INTRODUCTION

1 Intergovernmental Panel on Climate Change, 2007: Climate Change 2007: Synthesis report
2 Intergovernmental Panel on Climate Change, 2007: Climate Change 2007: Synthesis report
3 The Global Humanitarian Forum , 2009: Human Impact Report: Climate Change – The Anatomy of a Silent Crisis
4 United Nations Population Fund, 2007: State of the World Population 2007. Unleashing the Potential of Urban Growth
5 United Nations Human Settlement Programme, 2009: Cities and Climate Change Initiative. Launch and Conference Report
6 R. Fernandez- Castilla, L. Laski & S. Schellekens, 2008: Young People in an Urban World in G. Martine, G. McGranahan, M. Montgomery & R. Fernandez- Castilla (ed.), The New Global Frontier. Urbanization, Poverty and Environment in the 21st Century
7 R. Fernandez- Castilla, L. Laski & S. Schellekens, 2008: Young People in an Urban World in G. Martine, G. McGranahan, M. Montgomery & R. Fernandez- Castilla (ed.), The New Global Frontier. Urbanization, Poverty and Environment in the 21st Century

MARJORIE

1 Food and Agriculture Organization of the United Nations, 2009: State of World Fisheries and Aquaculture 2008
2 Bates, B.C., Z.W. Kundzewicz, S. Wu and J.P. Palutikof, Eds., 2008: Climate Change and Water. Technical Paper of the Intergovernmental Panel on Climate Change, IPCC Secretariat, Geneva
3 Dobson A, Cattadori I, Holt RD, Ostfeld RS, Keesing F, et al., 2006: Sacred Cows and Sympathetic Squirrels: The Importance of Biological Diversity to Human Health. PLoS Med 3(6): e231. doi:10.1371/journal.pmed.0030231
4 P. Hotez, A. Fenwick, L. Savioli, D. Molyneux, 2009: Rescuing the bottom billion through control of neglected tropical diseases, The Lancet, Volume 373, Issue 9674, Pages 1570-1575
5 International Labour Organization, 2009: Give Girls a Chance. Tackling Child Labour, a Key to the Future
6 United Nations Population Fund, 2007: Giving Girls Today & Tomorrow. Breaking the Cycle of Adolescent Pregnancy

MARIAMA

1 Intergovernmental Panel on Climate Change, 2007: Climate Change 2007: Synthesis report
2 Food and Agriculture Organization of the United Nations, 2003: Gender and Dryland Management
3 Food and Agriculture Organization of the United Nations, 2003: Gender and Dryland Management
4 International Fund for Agricultural Development, 2008: Desertification
5 International Fund for Agricultural Development, 2008: Desertification
6 United Nations Convention to Combat Desertification, 2008: Fact Sheet 3. The Consequences of Desertification
7 Food and Agriculture Organization of the United Nations, 2003: Gender and Dryland Management
8 Bates, B.C., Z.W. Kundzewicz, S. Wu and J.P. Palutikof, Eds., 2008: Climate Change and Water. Technical Paper of the Intergovernmental Panel on Climate Change, IPCC Secretariat, Geneva

MESSIAS

1 Food and Agriculture Organization of the United Nations, 2009: State of the World's Forests 2009
2 United Nations Economic and Social Council, 2009: Reversing the loss of forest cover, preventing forest degradation in all types of forests and combating desertification, including in low forest cover countries
3 Food and Agriculture Organization of the United Nations, 2009: State of the World's Forests 2009
4 Intergovernmental Panel on Climate Change, 2002: Climate Change and Biodiversity, IPCC Technical Paper V
5 Intergovernmental Panel on Climate Change, 2002: Climate Change and Biodiversity, IPCC Technical Paper V
6 Intergovernmental Panel on Climate Change, 2002: Climate Change and Biodiversity, IPCC Technical Paper V
7 Intergovernmental Panel on Climate Change, 2007: Climate Change 2007: Synthesis report, Summary for Policymakers
8 Food and Agriculture Organization of the United Nations, 2009: State of the World's Forests 2009
9 United Nations Forum on Forests (2009): Discussion paper contributed by the children and youth major group

KILOM

1 Bates, B.C., Z.W. Kundzewicz, S. Wu and J.P. Palutikof, Eds., 2008: Climate Change and Water. Technical Paper of the Intergovernmental Panel on Climate Change, IPCC Secretariat, Geneva, 210 pp.
2 Bates, B.C., Z.W. Kundzewicz, S. Wu and J.P. Palutikof, Eds., 2008: Climate Change and Water. Technical Paper of the Intergovernmental Panel on Climate Change, IPCC Secretariat, Geneva, 210 pp.
3 Francis X. Hezel, S.J., 2009: High Water in the Low Atolls, Micronesian Counselor - Issue 76. The Micronesian Seminar, Pohnpei
4 Bates, B.C., Z.W. Kundzewicz, S. Wu and J.P. Palutikof, Eds., 2008: Climate Change and Water. Technical Paper of the Intergovernmental Panel on Climate Change, IPCC Secretariat, Geneva, 210 pp.
5 Bates, B.C., Z.W. Kundzewicz, S. Wu and J.P. Palutikof, Eds., 2008: Climate Change and Water. Technical Paper of the Intergovernmental Panel on Climate Change, IPCC Secretariat, Geneva, 210 pp.

MANDISA

1 The Global Humanitarian Forum , 2009: Human Impact Report: Climate Change – The Anatomy of a Silent Crisis
2 Bates, B.C., Z.W. Kundzewicz, S. Wu and J.P. Palutikof, Eds., 2008: Climate Change and Water. Technical Paper of the Intergovernmental Panel on Climate Change, IPCC Secretariat, Geneva
3 Floods – Technical Hazard Sheet – Natural Disasters Profile, http://www.who.int/hac/tech-guidance/ems/floods/en/index.html, accessed 2009-06-27
4 Tropical Cyclones – Technical Hazard Sheet – Natural Disasters Profile, http://www.who.int/hac/techguidance/ems/tropical_cyclones/en/index.html, accessed 2009-06-27
5 Ramchandran,D. and Gardner, R., 2005: Coping with Crises: How Providers Can Meet Reproductive Health Needs in Crisis Situations. Population Reports, Series J, No. 53. Baltimore, Johns Hopkins Bloomberg School of Public Health, The INFO Project
6 Food and Agriculture Organization of the United Nations, 2006: Gender: The Missing Component of the Response to Climate Change

YOUNESS

1 E. Piguet, 2008: Climate Change and Forced Migration. Research Paper No. 153. United Nations High Commissioner for Refugees, Geneva.
2 International Organization for Migration, 2009: Policy Brief. Migration, Climate Change and the Environment
3 E. Piguet, 2008: Climate Change and Forced Migration. Research Paper No. 153. United Nations High Commissioner for Refugees, Geneva.
4 D. Kniveton, K. Schmidt-Verkerk, C. Smith and R. Black, 2008: Climate Change and Migration: Improving Methodologies to Estimate Flows. International Organization for Migration, Geneva
5 United Nations Population Fund, 2006: State of the World Population. A Passage to Hope. Women and International Migration

FATIMA

1 United Nations Framework Convention on Climate Change, 2007: Climate Change: Impacts, Vulnerabilities and Adaptation in Developing Countries
2 World Bank, UNDP et.al., 2003: Poverty and Climate Change. Reducing the Vulnerability of the Poor through Adaptation
3 Intergovernmental Panel on Climate Change, 2007: Climate Change 2007: Synthesis report
4 United Nations Framework Convention on Climate Change, 2007: Climate Change: Impacts, Vulnerabilities and Adaptation in Developing Countries
5 The Global Humanitarian Forum , 2009: Human Impact Report: Climate Change – The Anatomy of a Silent Crisis
6 United Nations Population Fund, 2007: The State of the World Population 2007: Growing Up Urban
7 United Nations Framework Convention on Climate Change, 2007: Climate Change: Impacts, Vulnerabilities and Adaptation in Developing Countries
8 United Nations Development Programme, 2008: The Millennium Development Goals report 2008